CW00432857

Content

Volume 97:3 Autumn 2007

Poems

Centrefold

Reviews

Endpapers

POEMS

ॐ

... the mighty angels of purgatory
who come solar-powered into darkness
using no other sails than their shining wings.
—*Alice Oswald*

Alice Oswald
Two Moon Poems

1. In A Tidal Valley

flat stone sometimes lit sometimes not
one among many moodswung creatures
that have settled in this beautiful
Uncountry of an Estuary

swans pitching your wings
in the reedy layby of a vacancy
where the house of the sea
can be set up quickly and taken down in an hour

all you flooded and stranded weeds whose workplace
is both a barren mud-site and a speeded up garden
full of lake-offerings and slabs of light
which then unwills itself listen

all you crabs in the dark alleys of the wall
all you mudswarms ranging up and down
I notice you are very alert and worn out
skulking about and grabbing what you can

listen this is not the ordinary surface river
this is not river at all this is something
like a huge repeating mechanism
banging and banging the jetty

very hard to define, most close in kind
to the mighty angels of purgatory
who come solar-powered into darkness
using no other sails than their shining wings

yes this is the Moon this hurrying
muscular unsolid unstillness
this endless wavering in whose engine
I too am living

2. Mud

this evening those very thin fence posts
struggled up out of the mud again
and immediately the meal began, there was
that flutter of white napkins of waders hurrying in

there was that bent old egret
prodding and poising his knife and fork
and so many mucous mudglands
so much soft throat sucking at my feet

I thought be careful this is deep mud this is
pure mouth it has such lip muscles
such a suction of wet kisses
the slightest contact clingfilms your hands

there goes that dunlin up to her chin in
the simmering dish of mush and
all night that seeping feeding sound
of moistness digesting smallness

and then I creep-slid out over the grey weed,
and all those slimy foodpods burst under me
I thought I know whose tongue I'm
treading on and under whose closed eye

every stone every shell every sock
every bone will be crammed in.
to my unease the meal went on and on
there were those queues of reeds

dipping their straws in the dead
there was that sly tide swiftly refilling
I thought really I should have webbed feet
I should have white wings to walk here

Jamie McKendrick
The Experiment

Ibn al-Haitham confirmed Ar-Razi's claim
The Eyes Are Not Radiators of Light
though Europe had to wait
five centuries till Kepler rightly guessed
the true function of the retina:
a small net, a cobweb tunic,
an exiled outcrop of the brain.

Scheiner the Jesuit whose nom de plume
was Appelles (draughtsman of the finest lines)
in 1625 was first to test
these theories on an ox's eye.
Cutting away sclera and choroid he left
the screen of the retina exposed and saw
the tiny wobbling world writ upside down.

It washed itself in a clear stream
when I drew a line across the white
– would that be the aqueous
or the vitreous humour
I wondered as the inner
architecture vanished in the flood:

the chamber walls, the measured dome
and the slow levels
like water-meadows at dusk
– all except for the pale lens, floating on light,
like a discus
made from bone and cloud.

The Critic Gets To Grips With Piero

Piero's numerous supporters keep
lavishing praise upon his "luminous brushwork"
but all that stuff about light's a red herring.
Half-blind, I'm sorry to say, and ecstatically blithering,
one of them even claims his Resurrection
is the great masterpiece of all time.
The other one has church bells on it.
Sure, no-one's saying the man can't paint trees,
horses and people. But can he do rocks?
The answer, I'm afraid, is no.
Are his rockscapes sexy like our Ruskin's –
seen (rooted, glistening) in and for themselves?
He seems to think all that's required
is the dull grey of a Franciscan cassock
arranged in vertical drapes like a curtain.
His rocks rise in these pitiful formations
around fictional scenes he's dreamt up
to please his patrons, things high on everyone's agenda
such as The History of the True Cross
(cue: the usual bigotry about the infidel).
He'll even paint his patrons in the foreground
which proves how servile and cliqueish he is.
He turns his rocks into a cursory backdrop
rather than what they are – various, intricate,
igneous, sedimentary, crystalline, smooth,
striated, whatever: the very basis of existence;
without which we'd be living in a swamp,
without which we might as well just give up
and go back to being fishes once again.
You'd have thought with all his vaunted
devotion to the Church – founded as we know
on Petrus etc. – he might have found
a spot of patient observation not so
ignoble. Is Tuscany really that shortchanged
on the rock front? – Ample opportunity, and what

does he come up with: dull, schematic stuff
worse than cement, gauche as papier-mâché
daubed with house paint for the school play.
And whilst I mentioned that his horses
have some merits ("moving softly, as though shod
in felt" as one exaggerated account would have it)
if you happen to be passing Arezzo
take a look at the squirrels he's done there –
they're nothing but a misbegotten cross
between rats and foxes – just a bushy tail
and the odd avidly clasped nut. Squirrels?!
They deserve better having supplied him
and his ilk for centuries with paintbrushes,
but these baleful creatures, bad as they are,
look almost lifelike put beside his rocks.
Will you look at them! He must have worked
really hard on the hopeless hog-tied things
especially for that wrapped-in-greasepaper-effect.

Martin Harrison
Plum Trees

What the plum trees were doing
was loading galaxies of flowers
like night sky's sprawling fire
in the middle of daylight.

Space turned into bloom and fruit.
Soil rose into juice and scent.
Electric, shaken, utterly still,
unpruned wands thirsted for Spring.

Like gluttons, the trees sucked everywhere
from hidden water, seemingly nowhere –
that was the ground inside the dark
as we walked dry earth, dead grass.

Unreasonably, not beyond forgetting,
it's that year's dry light which falls away
as if plum trees flare in unfenced shadow,
momentary as thought, or as a trace of thought.

Peter McDonald
The Interruption

Somebody almost takes the call
just when a phone stops; a slow
story is reaching the point, maybe,
while three or four others vacantly
wait for the spirit to move: but now
a story with nobody in it
barges straight in, in a flash,
before they can make themselves heard
or finish, before they can start.

Nobody says another word
as all of them hear the silence start;
they just take stock as if, oh,
they see now, and their faces fall.

August, 1998

The Reeds

On my own now with the lake, lake-water's
suck and slap against a wooden jetty
accompanies the solitary, middle-distance
heron that my eyes follow in its take-off
and heavy flight beyond their farthest reach.

I can walk for yards across these narrow planks
and touch the tops of reeds on either side
of me, where they come level with my arms:
the reeds move in the water as they give
under my hands, then come back to their places.

To see her arms and long wrists in the water,
her fingers slim and definite as reeds,
would be too much, and in the building quiet
admit that now, when nobody can hear,
it might be a relief to scream aloud.

As I turn towards the interrupted noise
where reeds are parting for me like a sea,
my heron circles back from the far shore,
aloof, but still checking on everything
in the water, to see what is really there.

Translations by Ali Alizadeh & John Kinsella

Mehdi Akhayan-Saales
The Return Of The Ravens

At the threshold of dusk
on a greying bay
a thousand black boats sail past.

No sunlight, no moon.
On the water's glistening surface
a thousand crooning black boats.

See how the scene changes colour
dark-hearted firmament and luminous star.
Engulfed in the pitch-black sea
crystalline islands appear to an observer
black patches on a white shirt.

A thousand fellow-travellers of a day's comings and goings
a thousand beaks having washed away the marks of work
a thousand tight-browed fellow-travellers and comrades
a thousand rotting corpses and remains.

On a greying bay
at a time when day
is what we call "the past", and night "the future"
at a time when the sky is lightless, and the moon
absent, I witnessed
black stars
flying through the pallid
firmament, noisy black stars
in that low and crowded pallid sky.

Attar
from The Conference of the Birds

> A wounded man was lamenting to a Sheikh.
Why are you crying? asked the Sheikh.
> O Sheikh, I have lost my beloved
Whose face transformed my world
> Her death killed me with sadness
The world blackened with loss.
> The Sheikh said: A heart made selfless
Will be your only recompense
> Another love will be bestowed on you
Who, deathless, won't inflict sadness on you
> A lover who feels robbed by death
Is one whose love brings grief to life
> A hundred afflictions will strike the face
Of whomever is struck by lust for a face.

My translation process begins with reading; not only engaging with the original poem in its linguistic genesis (Persian, in this case), but also 'reading' it in a critical sense, that is, contextualising, interpreting and analysing the text with the purpose of approaching its discursive formation. On the basis of this reading, I formulate the best English equals/equivalents of the Persian words in preparing a rough literal conversion. This draft, accompanied by additional notes regarding the specific stylistic and prosodic aspects of the original, is forwarded to John Kinsella for rewriting. Finally, I read his version against the original. *AA*

Latinate script languages are far easier for me to work with. I do not have Farsi, and find it hard to follow, and though I am learning as I go, and seeking to gain an understanding of the language, I am largely relying on Ali Alizadeh's literal English versions. But it's not simply a case of 'converting' this to an 'English-language' poem. There's clearly a process of collaboration: I ask Ali to send me the literal rendering, together with a commentary on the poem itself, on the poet, and any technical/prosodic peculiarities. Ali is a fine poet and an acute reader of poetry, and passionate about Persian/Iranian poetry. I also ask him to send me a copy of the original: I like not only to see the shape of the poem on the page, but to do my best with the script, and with understanding how it is working. It is also important for me to get historical and cultural contexts for the poem, whether of the past or contemporary. In the end, though, it is an inherent 'sense' of the poem that makes it work – some poems I cannot translate, others really find their mark with me. Once I have done my first version I send it back to Ali for comment. I enjoy working, though, and as someone with a bit of a 'history' background, I like to explore eras and contexts. *JK*

David Harsent:
Two Poems After Yannis Ritsos

Penelope

Not that she was fooled by his disguise:
she'd have known him by his scars for sure,
by the way he cast his eye over the dead
and dying suitors. What was there to say?
Twenty years of waking dreams... now here he stood
in the light from the dying fire,
a greybeard dappled with gore. 'Welcome,' she said,
in a voice she barely knew, he barely recognised.

Her loom cast latticed shadows on the ceiling;
the grave-cloth she'd worked to destroy
hung on the frame like something flayed.
Shapes in the weave darkened to ash
and lifted off, black birds of night
low on the skyline and disappearing fast.

The Acrobat

He walked on his hands, so perfectly upside-down
that he seemed to make past present, present past.

Then the floor opened and swallowed him.
We looked at each other: who would ever believe us?

A moment later, the doorbell rang.
There he stood, with a basket of oranges.

I first came across Yannis Ritsos's work in a translation by Alan Page,
published in pamphlet form by Ian Hamilton's *The Review*. This was 1969.
I thought the poems were exceptional: haunting, mysterious, visceral,
pitch-perfect. I'd had it at the back of my mind since then to make English
versions of Ritsos. I don't speak Greek. My method is to get, from several
sources, a strictly (one might say severely) literal version of the poem I
want to work on; also to look at several variant translations already done.
This approach is the one I adopted for my versions of Goran Simić's siege
poems; the idea is to make a version from the literal translation that
will be true to the spirit of the original but work as a new poem in
English. Will *read* as a new poem in English. I am prepared to be radical
in achieving this. This technique is nothing new and seems to me entirely
uncontroversial. *DH*

Inna Lisnianskaya, trans. Daniel Weissbort
from *Ekho*

In The Monastery Gardens

Stone and verdure of winding paths.
Rose pastures in the alleyways.
Granite chips in yellow slit-trenches,
In a foxhole of hills, a monastery.

In its refectory, earthenware crockery.
A narrow cell foretells superfluity
Of people. Where there's so little room,
Time, like a tree, grows upwards.

And a scarlet cloud, like a bush,
Ignites the moment of sunset.
I'm here by chance. A chip of granite,
like a tooth grown into the gum.

The tree's in the sky, in the mouth bitterness,
I recall the Russian tocsin of the rain;
What are you thinking, you who have
Not left home for a thousand years!

With my optic nerve,
I hook the nets of light,
Full of holes. In this world,
Nothing makes me weep.

The swan flaunts itself and
The carp's fins are silvery.
My thoughts stretch
Their wretched hands

Towards that light where you
Alone will notice:
The lower strata of the sky
Are mirror-like nets

Above the lake...

ℬ

Israel. February. Warmth.
The desert's yellow rose

The fields' crimson rose,
The sea's blue rose;

But as for the wind's roses,
No new symbol there.

Like the insistent chorus of days:
Israel. Warmth. Terror.

March One. Red Sea. Eilat.
The cards, as you can tell, have been propitious –
Enough of drabness – a brilliant sunrise
I am on the threshold
Of a flowering day.

The coral reef glows like a green rose,
Seaweed, wormlike, pouts,
Astonished at how lovely this world is:
Fish plumage is more colourful than the flowers.

Fish float. The transparent body of a tuna
Reminds me of a grey balloon,
Leisurely, like a merchant, casting an eye
Now on the local trollops, now his goods.

A yellow-winged fish, known as a butterfly,
Guides the tuna between the pink polyps.
"Catch me if you can!" it burbles.
In the crimson branch, water bluely gapes.

There, blushing like the branch
It's glued itself to, an octopus hides.
But who knows from whose eyes?
I try to sum it all up, try

But it can't be done. Like the seaweed,
I make so bold as to gape
At the unprecedented loveliness.

Shloma

Here it's only Shloma, the gardener, knows the flowers' names,
Shloma, casqued in grey curls, with a collar of beard:
Baby's breath, thorns, cloying straws,
Pollen too – a garden, after all!

The gardener is known not just to the hillsides of orchids,
Or to his own children – he's had four –
But to all of Judea's sweet-toothed bees –
Here there's a particular liking for brilliant flowers.

Also paint and brushes know the gardener,
And await him in the little hill house of canvas,
Because faces and leaves grow there
Like the days of the week, wonderful and simple.

And actually everything began with a hollow
Cry: in forty-five, his mother, pregant,
Escaped to freedom, leaving Mauritius, so the boy
Might be born in a garden as yet unplanted.

Translating poetry is, as Michael Hamburger titled his autobiography, repeating I believe what Eliot had said, "a mug's game". However, one often realizes this too late. Particularly impossible is the translation of lyric poetry, poetry of high verbal intensity, depending largely on the resonances of the source language. Lisnianskaya writes from deep within the Russian language and literary tradition, and her poems have a kind of aphoristic or folk intensity virtually impossible to reproduce. Like all good poets, however, she is also precise in her formulations and sometimes this can be conveyed. *DW*

Euripides, trans. Robin Robertson from *Medea*

lines 230–266

Medea:

[…]

Of all living, sentient creatures,
women are the most unfortunate.
We must save and save to raise a dowry;
then the man that agrees to marry us
becomes master of our bodies:
a second burden greater than the first.
Loss and insult: that is all we have.
Everything hangs on his character:
is the master good or bad?
We cannot refuse him anything, but if we divorce
we are seen as somehow soiled, as damaged goods.
Innocents and strangers, we enter our husbands' houses,
with all these new laws and customs to deal with;
we need to use our intuition to teach us
how best to please our man.
If we do well in all our duties, and don't let him
ever think he's imprisoned in the marriage,
everything's fine. If not, it's death in life.

When a man's bored of what he has at home
he goes elsewhere: finds someone else to amuse him.
The woman must wait, for she is allowed
to look at one face only: his.
Men tell us that we are lucky to live safe at home
while they take up their spears and go to war.
Well, that's a lie. I'd sooner stand behind a shield
three times in battle than give birth once.

But yours is a different story. This is your city.
Your fathers are here;
you have the pleasures of life,
the company of friends.
I am alone in Corinth, an outsider
in a strange city far from my family –
my only company a husband
who took me as plunder from some foreign campaign
and now dishonours me. I have no mother, no brother,
no kin to turn to, to shelter me from shame.
So I shall ask this one favour from you.
If I can think of any way, any plan,
to make my husband pay for all this hurt,
will you keep my secret?
A woman is too timid, too weak, they say, for war
– would faint at the sight of battle-steel –
but when she is injured in love,
when her bed has been defiled, she'll have your blood.

There are no manuscripts in the hand of Euripides or, indeed, any of the classical authors: the only complete transcriptions that survive are from the tenth century, and they are copies of copies. Over the centuries there have been ample opportunities for textual corruption, and texts of the play more academic than this one offer solutions of reconstruction 'by conjecture'. They also address the problem of interpolation, where new matter appears to have been added to expand or elaborate the original. I have used the Loeb Classical Library edition, edited and translated by David Kovacs, as my primary source, and have consulted a number of excellent English translations – primarily those by John Davie, Alistair Elliot, James Morwood and Philip Vellacott. My main concern has been to provide an English version that is as true to the Greek as it is to the way English is spoken now. *RR*

Sophocles, trans. Ruth Fainlight & Robert Littmann from *Antigone*

lines 1192–1243

(Messenger addresses Eurydice – who is Creon's wife, Haimon's mother, and would have been Antigone's mother-in-law. As always in Greek tragedy, violent action takes places off-stage, and is described by a Messenger.)

Messenger:

Dear mistress, I was there, and will describe
what I saw, leaving nothing out.
Why should I soothe you with words
later proved false? It is always better to tell the truth.
As his guide, I went with your husband
up to the furthest part of the plain where, still
unmourned, the body of Polyneices lay, ravaged by dogs.
We entreated Pluto, and the goddess of the crossroads,
to hold back their anger and show mercy.
We laved the remains with purifying water,
broke off branches to burn what was left
and heaped a high mound of his native earth
for a tomb. Then we turned towards the maiden's
stone-paved prison, the chamber of Hades' bride.
Already, from afar, one of us had heard
a wailing voice from that accursed place
and came to tell our master Creon.
The garbled anguished sounds grew louder
the nearer we approached. He also groaned
and loudly cried: "How wretched I am!
How could I foretell I was about to tread
the most unhappy path of all I've walked?
It is my son's voice that greets me! Servants,
hurry, closer, look – go to the tomb
where the stones that sealed its mouth were pulled away
and tell me if I am right to recognise that voice as Haimon's –

or if the gods deceive me."
Obeying our master's desperate commands
we went deeper into the tomb
and there beheld the girl – hung by the neck
in a noose of her linen veil –
and he, pressed close, clutching around her waist,
moaning and wailing the loss of his bride to the underworld,
the deeds of his father, and his doomed marriage.
When Creon saw him, a horrid cry burst from his lips
and he moved towards him, calling,
"Poor unhappy boy, what have you done?
What passed through your mind?
You have gone mad and destroyed yourself.
Come out, my child, I beg you."
But the boy glared at him wildly
and kept silent – then spat in his face
and drew his double-edged sword. When his father
ran to escape, the blow missed.
The doomed boy, furious with himself, curved
his body forward and thrust the sword deep into his own side.
Half-conscious, he lifted his weakened arms to embrace the girl
and choking, coughed a stream of blood onto her white cheek.
His corpse enfolding hers,
their marriage rites at last achieved in Hades –
a sight to demonstrate how lack of wisdom
is mankind's greatest curse.

I certainly could not have made this translation without the help of my collaborator – and its initiator – Robert Littman. As well as his almost word-for-word 'crib' and line-by-line notes, I also referred to many other versions. First I would read his, then the others – from the correct and good Victorian version by Jebb to the excellent but not very strict one by Fagles. Then I would go back to Robert's, read it again, and begin. It was hard but thrilling work. As he is Professor of Classics at the University of Hawaii, most of our exchanges were by e-mail, although we met a few times a year in London during the two or three years the job took. Our intention was to produce a version accurate enough to be acceptable for teaching, which could also stand as a piece of literature. We hope we have succeeded. *RF*

Janet Sutherland
Illumination

At dark all our houses are lit up
no one speaks   but of glory in light
whatever we are most afraid of

you'd lie naked and alone
under stars
they'd make you cry if you could

be adrift
spaced, faint, distant
from fear that lights us all

rush lamp, candle, bare electric bulb

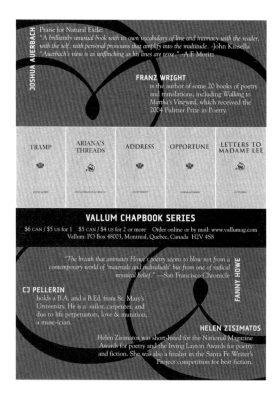

Adam Elgar
Ottavia

Stretch a spider's web a mile across the void
and plant an airy city on it, taut

between two peaks. Then you must creep
on wooden footways (minding the gap
and clinging to hempen handrails), gasp

at seductive deeps of nothing pulling at you,
(give or take a passing cloud or two)

and further than a lifetime's fall, the floor of the ravine...
Under the net hangs everything:
hammocks, gondolas, houses on a clothes-line,

fountains and football fields, a woman in a shower,
a farmyard, and a ballroom with a chandelier.

Vertiginous Ottavians feel no fear.
They know (unlike us) what their safety net will bear.

After Calvino, adapted from Le città sottili. *5*

E. A. Markham
Poem

Then someone looks up from her book to see an elephant in the garden.
That's what you need to restore the magic and mystery of literature
in these days of hardship. The poets of small titles are unnourishable, as we say,
as they allow no distraction or diversion to colour the verse:
things that get in the way of a slim idea's logic – too suggestive
of messiness in a life, or of a hinterland of experience too large for our time –
must be *genred* out. So frame after frame will be reduced in a game
where the detail is all, a bland pattern of syllables left to be admired.

So now we have it, a poem fit for today, the subject more or less solitary,
pondering the crossword of a life; being understated and stoic
about mishaps at the paths long taken; eschewing the vulgarity of old time
hero and anti-hero – oh, don't go there – for the more wearable badge
of victim: a shrewd assessment of the scribbler's small talent and rewards.
In this unenvied life I'm trying to smuggle the dream of earlier years,
of better titles, *The Princess of Cleves, The Old Curiosity Shop*,
and a place in your tight pentameter for a malignant dwarf called Daniel Quilp.

Apologies for disturbing the neat arrangement of words to admire,
words perhaps to console the sick, but sculptured like the shrinking self,
making the healthy and the living suspect blackmail: no one inside your poem
works through the backache, or has an adventure for the hell of it, or goes
to the loo. That's why I'm going to buck the trend and call this moment
not *A Princess of Cleves* or *An Old Curiosity Shop*, not even *A Bible*
or *A Koran*. But, thinking of that woman stirred by the elephant in her garden,
I'm going to call this arrangement of words, *Gulliver's Travels, II*.

Jane Draycott
Alpha

End of summer in the apartments.
On their rope-walks across the city
the dry months tauten to quiet.

At night, the ear gondolas through
the narrow echoing hours, the heart
slap-slapping under bridges
of sometimes only a single word.

Through the caverns of brickwork
we listen for vital signs – the man
below echo-finding on his radio,
a piano trickling with water,

winter with its chloroform mornings
pulsing hundreds of miles offshore:
begin, begin, begin.

Kate Bingham
August

August again
in a house in the country

here comes my childhood
wheat beet and barley

run like the wind
my daughters love me

let's play pretend
we all have the same mummy

she's wearing her apron
and cooking spaghetti

nothing we do
can make her be happy

grassflowers camomile
speedwell and poppy

wilt on the windowsill
scatter their debris

leave me myself again
faint faded dusty

running the tap
as the kettle boils empty

somewhere in earshot
the children abruptly

look up from their game
remember they're thirsty

David Morley
A Rainbow

The caravans' windows run with pre-rainbow light, that skyline twisting
to twine where the women of the gypsy camp sling their yellow washing.
Target-practice, they reckon, *for the village men, come the drinking hours.*
Washtubs, tail-chasing mutts, tail-spin car wrecks... The small change
of children spills from the indigo of shrubs, faces in the uplight violet
from their dad's roadside forges. Late, they run for the tin school-bus.
From the buds of their blowtorches, those fathers work written-off, rotten steel
until it's blue, hammerable – rattleable as a thunder-box – then slam it, red
                                                    into green
washing sluice, their children leaping through the steam as if they grew from it.

Andrew Fentham
Fowl Language

When a toe is stubbed
the head jerks and the elbows jut,

and with it, close to a cluck,
Fuck. Fuck. Fuck. Fuck.

Christopher Wallace-Crabbe
Turn Of The Screw

Toward the dot of setting Venus
early sparrows,
dusty little toughs,
try out a note or two.

If the news is bad
then it's called news,
but if not,
not.

There are days when weather forecasting
doesn't add up to
a hill of beans,
broad, French or kidney.

Looking at this morning's traffic
my late mother
would have smiled wanly and murmured,
"They've let them all out today."

You assume it's the Lebanese drivers
in shiny red cars
who muscle most anxiously,
roaring from lane to lane.

When we were all
chucked out of Paradise
the archangel apparently said
that work would save us

and the office desk welcomes you
like a littered paramour,
its computer face
shining with joy.

Beasts

Elastic, subtle, canny, rapid
or maybe merely dogged
which as the very word would suggest
    can apply to them all too well,
animals inhabit
another world of cognition

from you and me
(whatever you reckon
about the deep intellect
    of your siamese cat
which mainly behaves like a member
of your home team).

Agouti and antelope
are just not human at all,
though dolphins can sing along
    if not exactly in tune,
while the lion with its pelt of gold
simply exceeds us, a king.

Sheer glory, those muscles rippling
under a sleek pelt – for those
who respond to such beauty;
    we know too little
about the introspection
even of mares and stallions.

We are all tempted to say
that a dog could feel guilty:
our own Fido, at least.
    But envy? Or nostalgia?
And does the bounding leopard
rejoice in his great leap ?

Fred D'Aguiar
Subaltern

I missed my grandmother's funeral,
Missed too, Granddad's planting of a coconut
Grove to honour her memory, missed, in fact,
Her coming up as much as her going under,
If truth were told, since she lived more
Dead than when she breathed and walked
Boards I scrubbed with a scraper every Saturday
Morning in Airy Hall, an address we played with
Ad infinitum, *near Mahaicony, East Coast*
Demerara, Guyana, South America, Earth, her name
Uttered on more lips by people she birthed, washed,
Scolded, gave away or doused with a sponge all night
Through fever, shook awake from nightmares,
Accompanied in dreams of light that held sway
Over them like the hammock we christened
Yellow Submarine, made from stitched
Paddy bags and slung between two basement rafters,
We all piled into and rocked and sang '*We all live...*'

I pictured her grave one thousand different ways,
Until I clapped eyes on it and forgot all but one
Way of looking when laid to rest: her headstone,
Fifty yards behind the house, among coconut trees
Whose dry fruit crash-land unannounced,
Beside my grandfather, their hands, so I fancy,
Clasped across the divide, tunnelled in sleep
Far from light, from naked sight, heads turned
Sideways, seeing each other in a death stare,
Plastered smile, darkness-governed, stillness
For life and us above her and him keeping
What we know of the two on our breaths now,
Always, as if they cared enough to reach up,
Touch our bare feet when we passed with our heads
In the air, mindful of unhinged, dry coconuts.
Solar System, Milky Way, Galaxy, Universe...

The Return

for Ruby and Victor Ramraj

Whether Titta stands for sister or no
No more ice pick and its flint on the blockhead of ice

Whether Mama Dot stands for Grandma Dorothy or no
No more right hand cutlass swings at the left hand's juice and jelly

Whether Cooperative Republic village number 162 stands for Airy Hall or no
No more full-frontal kiss of cars on the pronounced curves of the S-road
That's the only road into town

Whether guinep or stinking-toe or sour-sop or jamoon stand for fruits or no
No more sprints from the house at the first smell of rain in nothing but our
                                                                    peeled skin

Whether to lime is to hang and to gaff or labrish is to shoot the breeze or no
No more shielding the wick of the oil lamp as I duck under the top half
While I toe open the bottom half of the back door's half-doors

Whether backdam stands for koker or no
No more going dutch for a day trip to Kyk-Over-Al
Where the Essequibo spreads like a sea
Where the Mazaruni and the Cuyuni part mineral company

Whether Kaictcur falls for a record 741-foot single drop or no
No more eye-turn, head-spin shuffle of up and down
So that the falls rise and the forest canopy bows to the floor

Whether Guyana is kanaima or no
Whether I-an-I stands for you and me or no

Alan Brownjohn
Ludbrooke

His Old Approach

Ludbrooke remembers saying to a girl
Watch this space! Which girl he can't recollect,
Or the space in which he planned to reapppear.
He seems to think it had been a time for action,
A time for trying out some new approach;
But his only action had been to bark *Watch this space!*
And smile, he hoped intriguingly, as he left her
– And was that enough to count as an "approach"?
Then whether he said it sober or after drinking
He is unsure. He keeps this metaphorical
Cabinet of approaches for future use.
How is it they gather dust even in the darkness
Of metal drawers too cumbersome to pull out?

His Linguistic Endeavours

Have included Luciana (foreign for "Lucy"),
Tempted out on a cloudy summer day
To a different cafeteria. Ludbrooke, buying
The coffee – and the croissant – or the sandwich
Tries (in her language!) to get her to compare it
With the one where she works. It's her day off,
And he calls this "your semi-liberation". She smiles
As he tries to find a favourable moment
For suggesting they go back to his flat,
And make this a "wholly liberated" day
Relaxing on his balcony, hearing him speak
Her language badly with an English charm
– Until, he hopes, the rain drives them indoors…

His Invention

On one occasion he has cooked rather well,
And she's actually eaten most of it for once.
There's a silence requiring something to be said,
– Or done, perhaps? He takes up her free hand
And, having tried this on himself, applies
The dried-with-his-upper-front-teeth tip of his tongue
Very delicately to the narrow gap between
The long nail and the skin of her middle finger,
While she sits and watches him, bemusedly.
This Ludbrooke gesture receives its première between
His main course of monkfish and his option
Of fresh fruit – or biscuits and mild cheddar.
When she takes back the tested finger and extends its hand
To a peach in his bowl, it's still too close to call.

His Classic Modesty

This is my bedroom, he says in a casual voice
And lo! My bed, below my photograph
Of the Acropolis. (*My love-making,* he thinks,
And sometimes even dares to say all this out loud)
Is like the Acropolis, an edifice
Wonderful to have experienced even once,
And transformative *to have known for a little longer.*
Sufficient of the Acropolis remains
In its incomparable magnificence
To stir a senstive girl for years to come.
Those who forego it weep at what they have missed
When their chance has vanished. And then he adds
Intelligent girls adore *the Acropolis.*

Thursday 31 January 2008, 7 p.m.

The Poetry Society Annual Lecture
with Eavan Boland
in association with Bishopsgate Institute

Shades & Contours: A Cartography of the State of Poetry

Eavan Boland has lived in Ireland, England and the United States and has, through a long and distinguished career as a leading poet of her generation, reflected, both in her art and in critical explorations, on the complex intersections and divergences between the language, meaning, history, inheritance, obligations and public functions of poetry on both sides of the Irish Sea and either side of the Atlantic.

The Poetry Society is privileged to have such a seminal explorer of life, of women's lives in particular, and of poetry in general in Britain and Ireland, and author of many collections including 'The Journey', 'Outside History' and 'The Lost Land', give the Society's annual lecture, and metaphorically map some of the geographical complexities and geological shifts that delineate the virtually unchartable landscape of poetry today.

The event will be introduced by Anne-Marie Fyfe.

Tickets: £12 (£8 concessions and Poetry Society members)
Venue: Bishopsgate Institute, 230 Bishopsgate, London EC2M 4QH
              www.bishopsgate.org.uk
To book: telephone 020 7392 9220

Thomas McCarthy
At Templemaurice House

In the beginning, light. At Templemaurice House,
Light in the cool dust of Nineteen Nineteen –
A grid of morning on the bare floorboards,
Oak light and ivy light, and the lead-crystal green

Of a Waterford demesne. Immense dreams
Coagulate around my fretting childhood heart:
My father dead in the Great War, lost Geraldine.
His books and manuscripts practise their art

Upon me and upon his loyal servant on earth,
My Uncle Walter. Dear bothered Captain FitzGerald
Paces the attic floor above me, learning poems
At dawn as he has always done; Wizard Earl

Of the Irish language, eccentric patron of the House.
A language. A poem. A Captain's drum-beat stirs,
Disturbs the dust. The grandeur of the world
Enfolds me still. Immensities. Cries. Open doors

And doors closing in the long corridor, the sound
Of water tanks replenished, the rasp of fire grates,
Mrs. Norah Foley's bicycle in the cobbled yard.
Urgency. Maura's frightened laying of plates –

Ah. I turn in my bed against the full light of day
Like any Irish child spoilt in the motherhood of war.
The U-boat of the hour has passed taking my father,
But I have begun again as the child of Uncle Walter,

Learning Irish faster than he ever could, the *Modh*
And *Tuisil* call me to themselves, but vex him still.
In the beginning, the immense light of poetry,
The long immortal grid of light from Dromana Hill

That emblazoned the first hour of each private day.
Not simple. Not that. The light shone down upon us
Peculiarly even then: Anglo-Irish light
That shone on Usshers, FitzGeralds, Chearnleys, River Finnisk,

Blackwater and Bride, Dromana and Templemaurice.
In childhood's bedroom, a kind of waiting place,
All the material of what might ever be rushes in;
Poems, fathers, history and breakfast, all find space

And I sing beside them; hum and sing again
My uncle's macaronic anthem, *Na Connerys*:
Too young to know the troubles, Fenian or Raparee,
Yet I've gauged the ambient temperature, find ease

In song as if my Geraldine soul was born again
And hidden now in the culvert of a bedroom.
Under bedclothes the diffused light, and all
Bearable things; mother of the house, the womb.

Strange how a boy of nine, hiding naked in dawn
Happiness of himself, how such a lizard creature
Can see the whole of history. Clairvoyant is
Childhood, and complete is the soul's future

In a boy who has buried the father of himself.
The long day goes singing away from me, *tabhair*
Fuascailt orainn araon, like a convict in a convict-ship:
It is the future I must wake to see, to see its power

Racing across the twenty acre field beneath my room,
Down to the wide Blackwater, the liberating sea.
I part the bedclothes as I parted cold watercress
To slake my thirst. Surface. Norah Foley calling me,

Calling the entire household, but by proxy, with Maura's
Nervous tinkling, an Alpine cow-bell in the wide hall.
In ten minutes we will have assembled by the long table,
Uncle Walter and I, my mother, my sister Nesta, full

Of youthful gossip from her picnic at Glenshelane,
Her dream Lieutenants, her art class at the Misses Keanes.
For half an hour Mrs Norah Foley will cede her warm kingdom
With a pretence of work outdoors: she succumbed to a whim

Of my war-wounded Uncle, allowing the 'quality' to dine
In her kitchen; a kindness that is hidden from each
Big House that corresponds with us from far and near.
Maura serves in silence, with Mrs. Foley out of reach

And out of ear-shot. Only when Uncle Walter primes
With his sword stick the cobble of the yard does she
Appear once more, armed with a trug of potatoes,
With prodigious leeks, dark chives and fresh-cut parsley.

Deep childhood. Dreams. An older sister to take all the blame:
I was as spoilt a boy as was ever born near Cappoquin,
Retained at the farm, tutored by devoted women, enthralled
By a Captain parcelled home from war, never to leave again.

Templemaurice seemed to dream through me, as Uncle Walter
Did, thrilled by my love of words, of verbs and conjugations:
As months passed in slow time, pictures from *Illustrated War
News* torn down to make way for old poems of *The Nation*

And inexorably a kind of nation was given birth each time
My Uncle, after breakfast, recited a mysterious *Eriu* poem.
Here in the House I made a kingdom of Cuchulainn and
My kinsman, the Wizard Earl. Kuno Meyer and I shared a throne,

With my Uncle as faithful Chancellor. I could hear a deer's cry
And the blackbird in the wood, the monk snoring loudly
And the cock's persistent crow. Each translated image was
A subject that I could see, a deer or a blackbird breaking free.

Add salt to our History, pepper the memoirs of the well-fed;
History is no vichyssoise, so be sparing with the cream.
Heat the butter until it foams, Mrs Norah Foley said,
Add the chopped nettles in memory of our millions dead.

It is late springtime in the Templemaurice household,
Yellow house in a flood plain by a tidal river at Old Affane.
My Uncle Walter has caught the first trout of the season,
Fish speckled and delicate in his outstretched adult palm.

Mrs Norah Foley and my mother pace a floor that's cold as slate,
Happy with the glossy greens, adding freckled, first potatoes,
Covering the morning talk of Cappoquin with chicken stock,
Settling the story of each family, stacking them in neat rows

Like my uncle's fresh caught rainbow trout on the grill.
It is the before-summer of prodigious, elemental growth –
Even my uncle's words flick with a last gasp in the summerhouse;
Salt and words, pepper and poems complete our May-time meal.

Far away in the mist are the chopped scallions of roof-tops,
Farther in their ordinariness from what is happening at home:
Salt and pepper of the Irish language, exceptional love-poems,
'Bush-citadels in grey hood'. Uncle reads James Kearney's poem

For he and Mr. Percy Ussher are trawling in the tide of Irish,
Swopping Kearney and Kuno Meyer in the snug at Russell's shop.
Along the narrow corridor, between kitchen proper and cobble yard
I retrace the footsteps of the family with a child's reversed walk.

Vernon Scannell
Still Life

A plum, a pear and a pomegranate
with hard and polished skin announce
their presences on that white plate
resting on the wooden chair
beneath the baffled window where
a purple curtain softly falls
in sumptuous folds. The bloom of plum,
the yellow-speckled pear and shine
of pomegranate's hint of gold
are unrelated yet aware
of how the dull wood of the chair
is something wholly other than
the otherness of each of them.

Their stillness whispers of a dance
no lilting limbs have yet performed
to music never sung or played,
a seen sonata, tune of shapes,
an unimperilled quietude.

A Long-Distance Friendship

In May this year, *writes Eva Salzman*, the talented poet Sarah Hannah, a close friend, died tragically, and tragically young. She was an extraordinary person too, someone who called it as she saw it. Funny, warm, cynical, lyrical, she was both fragile and powerful, a combination of such extremes in equal measure, and smart as hell. The loss to the literary world is great. The loss to me is profound, unspeakable. When not engaged in high-brow literature, Sarah Hannah played guitar in a heavy metal band, and was once kissed by three out of the four Monkees. Ah well, nobody's perfect. Nobody could have been loved more. But she should have been read more during her lifetime. Read her now.

Sarah Hannah
The Missing Ingredient

Sixty-eight, or 'nine, when I was three or two, Paul Mariat harpsichorded "Love is Blue."
Everything a seamless paisley, sunflowered, serene; my father swears "Even
Renee was happy then." Indeed, all serums seemed to flow; housewives read the
Rubaiyat of Omar Khayyam (I have her copy), thought of eros, donned loose
                                                            multi-colored
Tunics. There she stands, still, true as Kodak, smiling, leaded casement window
On her left, walnut bookshelves on her right (visible title: *The Hinge of Fate*).
Neighbors (actual surname: Hamilton) farmed root vegetables, piled bees
In apiaries; we stood before the swarm and stared. So, was it all rot? Certainly
Not. I have stacks of photographic proof, just not enough oomph, not enough juice.

Blessed Thistle (*Cnicus benedictus*)

Let's go ahead and bless these double crosses,
These leaves about to stick us in a hundred places;

It's purported to protect from evil, plague, and harm,
And, according to the Bard, "it is the only thing for a qualm."

"Get you some of this and lay it to your heart," while
I run around and say some kind of benediction, try to smile.

Or maybe I'll grind it, make an herbal tea called Mother's Milk
For sale in California, or simply tear apart a thorny stalk,

Run it through my hand, draw it 'cross my wrist,
And make some sign, above the bed, to hold you fast –

Some auspicious symbol made of thorny English dross and blood
(To you, a dram of anything from England must be good) –

To scare away what makes you cry for help,
What makes you call out Mum! and keep

You a bit longer, breathing here with me.

Eva Salzman
Seas

for Leland Bardwell

Tell me the water's cold
I'll put myself on trial

this brief report
and I slip off my shoes

wade into pebbled fonts
left by low tide
to test the bite the burns

steel bolts shot
through the ankle

because
        I don't know

it's small but strong
towards triumph

a scrap of seaweed's
languid curl
around the foot

the flicker of fish
browsing creatures
nudged aside

                (ah, invisible sting
of the underworld)

evidence of daring
dark forbidding elements

with clenched teeth
the body lowering

                    slow and just so

it's only waist-deep brine
hands steering
slippery stones

it's just a swim
in quiet shoals

it's the full immersion

iced skin
        bone aches
electric

shocks from these
           odd needs

from freezing water freezing
bitter cold
so cold

at last
        I've found it
                yes feel it now I do

the warmth of humanity

Kit Fan
The Hairdresser By The Styx

Don't ask for a second chance: it is a relief
to live the same life again. What is beautiful
in repetition is not the false belief
in suffering, nor something as simple
as pure coincidence. All the things
that I saw, heard, breathed, touched, and ate.
For instance, an instant. All the beings
that I met I meet again. Some are late,
others early. In a story like this, I can't bear
to imagine the difference between the past
and the future. It is not present here.
Everything is the same and all is not lost.
Trust me, I spent most of my life in the mirror.
I do partings well. Loosen the tie. Undo the collar.

Catullus, trans. Simon Smith
85.

I loath and I love. You maybe want to ask why.
    I can't tell. It's under my skin and I'm wracked.

Ros Barber
Driving Without Lights

Dark road. Not even moonlight
spilling its ministry over the lip
of the kerb, and she switches off.

Tyres gasp, hug tarmac
as cats eyes close,
blinding the corners.

This thin, she could go anywhere.
Halve the breath between
oncoming juggernauts, slip

between atoms, the rapid alarm
of her pulse beating her back to a past
where she couldn't be good enough.

Now she's a wonder,
miraculously missing
the things she can't see:

looming verges snapped off
like safety tabs, pylons scarpered,
rabbits invisible sentinels

in the black of the land.
Regular telegraph poles
her waist is smaller than

swish past in the dark
like the hated days.
She's fast.

Until her eyes adjust,
nothing can touch her.
She's put out existence.

John Whitworth
Love Sonnet

The fat clock ticks and ticks and ticks and tells
Me stuff I didn't want to know I knew.
Across a million billion windowsills
The stellar dust is whispering of you.
A Balkan website that I can't access
Texts messages to the Uranian rings.
Since Tuesday last American Express
Are threatening unimaginable things.
A fairy child with an enormous head,
A forky tail and huge, prehensile claws,
Is swinging at the bottom of my bed
And doesn't seem to want to stay indoors.
Call me. I'm waiting for your call. What's done
Is done. There's nothing here for anyone.

Catullus, trans. Simon Smith
94.

Nob of knobs fucks. Fucking nob of knobs? That's for sure
   The saying goes: if the root fits pot it.

Peter Bland
SS Film Of A Village Clearance –
Poland 1943

A man is running towards his death
afraid of being late, of upsetting
the men with dogs and guns
who've already killed those who dug his grave,
rolling them into that pit...

                    It fades,
this scene, just before he's shot,
reversing itself, going back to the top
where he leaps, stark-naked, from the back of a truck
to begin his last journey up a bare slope
towards that brutal stop.

                  Hundreds more
are waiting in the shivering cold
but his is the image that never ends,
his is the crossing point, his is the look
of the last man on earth with nowhere to go,
his is that anxious stumbling trot.

Catullus, trans. Simon Smith
93.

I'm not much interested, Caesar, placating you,
   Nor bothered which side you're batting for.

Carrie Etter
Biopsy

This is my body. This is my heart,
standing aside like a child at the zoo.

What thrives behind those rocks, those bars?
It has a name I can't pronounce.

Neither swift nor sluggish, it's
the child I myself have borne.

There is no one else to apologise to –
I'm sorry, I'm sorry – it could be a lullaby

if my breast were not both
body and heart.

Nigel McLoughlin
Chorus

A thousand webs barely contain the green thrum
of the hedge and the night-drop dregs of silver
burst in the mouth; reek like zest. The eye irradiates
with a clamour of birds blackening into horizon.
Colour begins a slow thunder across the sky, multiplies
and changes; sings in bird-throat to the beat of wings.
The air hives with birth, vibrates out of shadow.
Everything burns, everything rings, including me.

The great bell of the world vibrates and I am drunk
with winter-shine. The concrete blazes. The red tang
of seven o'clock and the vein-belt of walking brazen
to the frost leaps through me. An hour before petrol-stink
and the shrink of people diminishing into a rush, here
in the open-throated song of morning, I am in the clear.

Charles Tomlinson

We celebrate Charles Tomlinson's anniversary year with these poems and with an interview in the next issue.

Handel Blind

Candle-light is not kind
to eyes that copy, compose by night:
it leads through the tunnel where
the near no longer exists
and only the ear can go,
searching-out still those sounds
that fill the grateful mind:
blind fingers now
repeat the lesson they knew by sight and now
by the braille of conviction:
let him stay seated here
where he can dictate
the point and counterpoint of conviction
crossing the dark.

To A Surgeon

Every vista that I see
Bears the scar you left in me –
Left on the eye beneath your knife
That cuts so deep into a life.

CENTREFOLD

ɞ

For me, a poem is a place where one invites someone in. You build a little house, fix it all up real nice. Inside, you've got some interesting things you want to show them.

—*Charles Simic*

The Lyric Principle:
Part 2: The Sound Of Sense[1]

DON PATERSON

Perhaps it's best to preface this essay on lyric technique with a summary of the main points I tried to argue in part one. After a discussion of the mnemonic function of poetry, I made the following observations:

1) *Language is a poetic system. When language is subjected to formal pressure and emotional heat, poetry is the natural result.*

2) *Language consists of sound-signs, and while their acoustic and semantic aspects may be separately described, they are not actually separable.*

3) *The corollary of this statement is that language operates on a principle of iconicity, that is to say: things sound like the things they mean. They do this through a hidden rule of synaesthetic representation. The mechanism of this iconic system is complex.*

4) *Poetry is a mode of language which, among other deviations from prosaic norms, sees a natural shift of emphasis from denotative to connotative meaning in its pursuit of brief expression. In a constrained space, connotative speech is far more economical and effective than denotative speech in suggesting the complex relations needed to unify poetry's often disparate and contradictory materials – it being in the imaginative connection of apparently contrary, unrelated or incompatible thematic elements that poetry often finds its 'epiphanies'.*

5) *As an immediate result of this connotative shift, poetry instinctively reaches towards the deliberate manipulation and intensification of the iconic or 'phonosemantic' system. Poets can trust their ears to think and their brains to listen; no compromise between sound and sense need be negotiated, as they are understood as aspects of the same thing. The negotiation lies between the sound and sense we intended to make, and the sound and sense we end up making; the gap between them defines the compositional process.*

6) *Within the special rules of poetry – which poet and reader are complicit in maintaining – unified sound is a* literal *and not symbolic means of unifying sense.*[2]

Poetry, I think, proceeds not from a selfish but a generous instinct. Whatever inner tensions have been assuaged in our writing, we want to give these things away in the end. To have someone else want your poem for themselves, it must be desirable; to be desirable, it must be – in the

---

1. Might as well start with a footnote. No, I don't mean quite the same thing as Frost, who used the phrase more generally to describe syntax as well as tone, and the poem as "talk-song".
2. This statement has many strange corollaries. To give one: a poem which deliberately sought to exhibit no patterning would also be engaged in a simultaneous project of sense-dismantling.

broadest sense – beautiful; and for a reader to find it beautiful, it must exhibit some of the symmetry we find in the natural. (By "symmetry" I don't merely symmetry of form.) This last might seem a bit of a leap, though it's as old-school as it comes, of course: it's been a cliché since Plato and Aristotle to say that the reason we find a piece of art satisfying is because it is "imitative of nature"[3]. I still like to think of a poem as kind of a man-made natural object, our 'best effort', that we quietly slip back into the world, and to which the world can make no serious objection.

Poetry is often compared to music, but most of the comparisons are pretty facile, or plain false. In one important way, however, I think they're closely analogous processes. If we define music as those sustained noises that we consensually agree make satisfying or emotionally meaningful arrangements of sound, when we examine such a noise, and look at the way that one note-event follows another, we find that their sequenced patterns converge on the same fractal statistic[4] that we find in natural dynamic systems – everything from quasar emissions to river discharge, traffic flow, sunspot activity and DNA sequences. It is something often referred to as 'pink noise'. This is neither 'white noise' (in acoustics, it's that *shhhh* sound where all frequencies are heard simultaneously, at equal power) where the relation between one note and the next is uncorrelated and completely random); nor is it correlated 'brown' or – more accurately – 'Brownian noise', where pitch of the next note is decided wholly on the position of the previous one, through the application of an inflexible rule. Music generated on a white noise algorithm is ugly in its unpredictability, and Brownian just as so in its predictability. But if we hit upon something in between, something 'pink', we find it beautiful: in other words, something that corresponds to our ideal balance of predictable regularity and surprise.

While analyses of static forms in nature – the outline of a landscape, for example – reveal correlated Brownian patterns[5], when it comes to natural dynamic processes we find pink noise dominating; it appears to be the characteristic signature of complex systems, i.e. those which display non-random variation. The changing content of our sensory experience seems to hover around the pink noise mark; this sensory music is as much a product

---

3. The occasional use of the phrase 'organic verse' for 'free verse' is just substituting an error – a pretty stupid one – for a misnomer. In the organic, symmetry is everywhere. Once wholly 'freed' from every aspect of formal patterning, a poem may indeed be 'organic', but only like some kind of diseased amoeba. A better defence of faith-based free verse practice is the Lawrentian argument that it more closely represents the dynamic shape of spontaneous thought; but even this tends to ignore the fact that thought itself is highly rhythmic – and that spontaneous thoughts are often the least original we have. The 'flash of inspiration', welcome as it is, has given spontaneity an undeservedly good name. First thought = worst thought, speaking personally.
4. The $1/f$ ratio of spectral density.
5. Perhaps an explanation why we find Brownian noise acceptable in static visual art, but not in dynamic time-based art; the static and visual aspect of poetry – its typographic arrangement on the page – is tellingly 'correlated' in its stanzaic and lineated symmetries, however.

of the nervous system as of nature – the *input* received at our physical extremities can be near-chaotic white noise, but our brains filter it down to pink, screening out the irrelevant noisy data, and leaving only those patterns of change which have become useful to our specific evolved intelligence. The wholly dynamic, time-based medium of music is dominated by this, and the pattern of regularity and variation in its pitch and volume (just like human speech, incidentally) matches perhaps more perfectly than any other kind of art the spectral density of our flickering perception of the world.

It seems reasonable to assume that our brains also perceive the dynamic system of the successful poem as similarly balanced. (The poem *itself* can be thought of as operating, in its way, like a miniature nervous system, screening the pink noise of our perception even further, leaving only a pattern of locally significant data.) The best poetry has nothing so easily measurable as note pitch and length, however, but I'd suggest that were we able to accurately measure its concrete and abstract speech, its light and dense lines, the pattern of its metrical agreement and disagreement, we would see something identical emerge: an honourable echo of nature, of its balance of correlated and uncorrelated, of randomness and self-similarity.[6] And, perhaps, its most crucial equilibrium: that of predictability and

---

6. Were we really able to measure those things accurately, there would be nothing to stop us automating the process. While I believe that one day it will be entirely possible to write a great poem with a computer, we will probably have already 'gone biotech' by then, and begun the smart move from carbon to silicon – in which case it won't seem such a big deal to our bionic scions. (Indeed such an elusive poetic algorithm already seems to exist in our wet brains, and it doesn't seem miraculous or impossible to us: it probably should.) We are far closer to devising such a thing for music, though, and the fact that poetry and music are comparable systems seems to suggest that we only lack a proper description of our own compositional process. The perennial fear is that the work would shed its 'humanity' – but one only has to look at the way traditional music skills have been ported over to programming to see those fears are quite unfounded. On the contrary – programmers invest their music with as much humanity and human expression as any other language, and the laptop turns out to be as humanly responsive as any other instrument. (Paradoxically the necessity of *programming* in the humanity has led to a bizarre expertise in the expressive exaggeration of human error: computer-based music is already in its Romantic phase.) The fear is just the standard wariness over new means of production: similar misgivings were initially voiced over cameras, typewriters, the pianoforte and the printing of books themselves. There is no good reason why computers should not soon be useful to our art. Generative music programming – essentially the art of judiciously modulating white noise aleatoric data with some brown noise rules to produce something delightfully 'pink' – is fairly close to providing some very decent music, and reminds us that Bach's genius was computational as well as inspirational. Poetry is a vastly more complex business only because its listable parameters are far, far more numerous, but not – who would seriously claim this – because it captures any more of the human spirit than does music. Current efforts at generative poetry are still aspiring to the merely daft, and most depend upon stochastic algorithms to produce surreal effects of the "fatuous banana spliced my windmill" variety – which appear 'poetic' only because nonsensical linguistic input overstimulates our connecting faculties. Poets, needless to say, have had nothing to do with their programming. An algorithm for poetry would be incredibly complex, but not infinitely so; and its detachment from such overvalued and sentimental constructs as 'the individual voice' could be just the thing to propel us into a new era of Classicism, should we desire or require such a thing.

surprise, the familiar and the unfamiliar, the known and the unknown. Wholly familiar 'Brownian' poetry consists in the mere rehearsal of what the poet (and usually the reader) already know to be the case, and unfolds in a wholly predictable manner; it fails because it doesn't surprise. 'White' poetry is all unfamiliarity and novelty and discontinuity, and fails because it does nothing *but* surprise. (This sounds just dandy, until we consider that there is nothing so predictably dull as an infinite series of exceptions). If our aim really is epiphany, the poem must demonstrate a move from the known to the unknown, an uncorrelated leap from a correlated position; but it can only do so by actually *making* it – and therein lies the risk and seriousness of our word-game.

Of course there is a musical balance to be achieved too. Poetry *naturally* refines the music of language to something pink – something correlated, modulated by something variable – and it's that mechanism I'll spend the rest of this essay discussing. Poetry achieves a balance of shifting vowel and echoed consonant, of airy music and stop-heavy music that is, perhaps more than any other physical property it exhibits, the truest emblem of its natural art.

ℬ

One of those hellish things you learn after ten years working in editing – I hardly dare confess this – is that you can hold a poem a yard away, and without having read a word, know there's a 99% chance that you won't like it. Most often this is because any random two- or three-line passage appears to contain all the letters of the alphabet. (Centred text, copperplate fonts and falling bits of potpourri are also excellent pointers.) This means the poem is unlikely to have any music. The phenomenon of 'music' in poetry is often spoken about as if it were a mysterious quality; but if we mean 'music' as in 'music', rather than 'some ineffable thing which my poetic intuition can subjectively divine, but is beyond human articulation', it's actually very simply characterised. Except in some very particular cases, it means that the poem displays deliberate organisation and some form of symmetry or parallelism in its arrangement of sound. If a 'music' is ascribed to a poem, but cannot be described through pointing to some parallel phonic effect (or – stretching the definition to its limit – a patterned silence), the only music the listener has identified is that which resides naturally in the language itself.

The error is often made because this language-music is not inconsiderable. Even in everyday speech, given a choice of synonyms, we will express an unconscious preference for the more harmonious (i.e. the contextually lyric) sound when we need to make strong sense. This effect is naturally strengthened the more considered our speech, and speech-writers alliterate and assonate almost helplessly; written prose betrays a higher degree of lyric patterning again – and poetry, of course, even more so. (The self-conscious foregrounding of this patterning in prose is what – next to a lingering over description – most often leads to the equivocal diagnosis of 'poetic' writing.) But even a random series of words will appear to demonstrate a musical coherence simply by virtue of any one language being a closed phonemic system, and having a finite set of sounds it can combine.[7] Each language uses only a fraction of the possible sounds that human voice can produce; English does remarkably well – of the 200-odd phonemes in global use, it manages around 50. We might pity the native Hawaiian speaker with their mere 13, but a poet would sensibly envy them. When you think about it, it must be an effort to speak a sentence in Hawaiian that is not lyrically coherent.

Nonetheless, even without salient sound effects like rhyme, assonance or alliteration to point to, we often have the strong sense that something is going on beside the mere intrinsic musicality of the language; and indeed there is.

In English poetry, the feeling that a piece of writing is 'musical' usually means that it quietly exhibits two kinds of phonetic bias. Between them they represent the repetition and variation, the similarity and difference (the motif the human brain craves in everything it perceives, if it is simultaneously to make both connections and distinctions) that we find in every aspect of poetic composition. I'll name them now, and expand on them later. The first is the deliberate variation of vowel sounds; the second is consonantal patterning.

Between them, these two tendencies have come to represent an unconscious 'lyric ideal' in English. Importantly they must be *no more* than tendencies. Generally speaking, if sound-patterning is too strong, too conspicuous, it will be perceived as contrived, and distract from the sense – open Edith Sitwell's *Collected Poems* at random, if you want to see what I mean – unless it performs some explicit mnemonic or structural function, like Anglo-Saxon alliteration or terminal rhyme. (These *are*, in a way, perceived as contrivances – but they are passed over as the age's agreed modes of poetic artifice, the conventions of the poem's expert making, their invisible fashions.) A normative shift towards vowel heterophony and

---

7. This is the 'musicality' we quickly divine in languages or dialects we have trouble understanding (but are slow to acknowledge in our own); left to focus on the sound, we can attend to their pure music – hence the apparently infinite suggestiveness of their song-lyrics in those languages. Someone once asked me to comment on that cut-up collage stuff you get with your spam-mail, saying how beautiful and close to poetry some of it sounded. The trouble is that any old random garbage often strikes us as beautiful and poetic: this, however, pays a compliment to language itself, not to the poem. In such circumstances, having little in the way of conventional meaning to distract us, we can attend to the sound alone, and enjoy the distinctive gabble of the Anglophone.

consonantal homophony creates the unconsciously experienced 'lyric ground', above which the consciously-registered saliences of rhyme, assonance and alliteration can cleanly stand. Just as we see a global shift from denotative to connotative speech in the poem, so we see (concomitantly, bootstrapped from the phonosemantic system) a global shift from an inchoate language-music to an explicit poetry-music. All poets with half an ear default to the lyric ground more or less all the time; it is, in effect, the poet's working medium, the canvas, clay and stone from which they carve out the poem.

In the human voice, the vowel carries the bulk of the feeling in its complex tonal and quantitative discriminations, while the consonants which interrupt that breath makes the bulk of the sense. The consonant, in making the distinction between *blue* and *shoe* and *true*, gives the phonetic differentiation we need to have a sign-system capable of carrying distinct meanings; the envelopes with which it shapes the vowel allow for discrete words to be heard, in much the same way that physical borders allow us to perceive discrete objects. The material basis of that sign-system, though, is the voiced breath. Vowel fills the word with its fairly uniform stuff, while the consonant carves it into recognizable shapes. Consider, say, a mother's frustrated demand to her child, "put down the cup." It's easy to separate out the four vowels | ʊ | aʊ | ɪ | ʌ | ('oo – ow – ih – uh') then imagine the first vowel pitched high to indicate urgency, the second dipping down an interval of a fifth or sixth to reinforce the impression of sane control, the third pitched identically to the first to reinforce the imperative, and the last rising another fifth – and increased in loudness – to convey the non-negotiability and frustration of the demand. The emotional sense would be clear from such a performed sequence of tones, if not the literal sense; but the consonants *pt dn th cp* alone will give us a fair stab at the semantic content, if not the tonal shape. (Note that with the consonants removed, speech suddenly becomes an extremely complex kind of singing.)

In the non-performative context of written language, however, things are trickier. Try all the different ways you can pitch "I love you", if you want to demonstrate the hopelessly attenuated emotional palette of written speech; spoken, it's easy to draw out shades of meaning that are alternately questioning, pleading, heartfelt, insecure, angry, desperate, tender, insincere, placatory and so on, just by modifying the song of the vowels. In written language, the performative cues have to be given by interpreted sense; this is provided in a thousand different ways, but phonically, it's something delegated largely to the consonant. Because written speech doesn't represent the pitch- and length-patterns that give it its expressive range, it's easy for the vowel to become devalued – to the extent that some graphic systems have done without it altogether. Poetry, in declaring itself as emotional, urgent speech, and in signing its kinship with song, puts the vowel back centre-stage. How does it do this?

Because vowels have perceptible duration, they are easy to hear. You can test this by trying to repeat the vowel sounds in the previous sentence; you should be able to do so almost thoughtlessly, and just repeat the sentence as a form of de-consonated babytalk. *Because vowels have duration they are easy to hear:* ə `ɔ | `aʊ ə | æ | ʊ `a ə | eɪ | æ | `ɪ ɪ | ʊ | ɪ | – or something like it. Now try and do the same with the consonants. It's almost impossible without thinking about it very carefully. The vowel is the main durational component of the word; the consonant we often experience as temporally negligible. From here it's a short imaginative leap to 'timeless', and it's interesting to note that those languages whose writing systems omit vowels – Egyptian hieroglyphs, Hebrew and Classical Arabic – have found it easy to sustain the idea of a holy book that had existed before the dawn of time, and, as it were, fell to earth as a block of eternal and monolithic consonant, into which the impure, sour breath of the human had not yet been introduced. Both the Torah and early versions of the Koran were written without vowels or diacritical marks, and both the Kabbalists and Sufis were both engaged in the mystical project of re-envowelling their holy books in order to come up with alternative, deeper interpretations in addition to the 'standard' reading; in this way, they could intuit the secret intentions of the Divine. (This is a riff of which I've become overly fond, but briefly: their researches are almost procedurally identical to what we call pararhyme, where words with the same consonantal structure are sought out by choosing a word, removing the vowels and then re-envowelling it to generate a secret cognate, or a whole series of them. These are then used as a means of interrogating the memory and imagination, which must then link them up as stations in a intelligible narrative: essentially it treats the mind as if it were a holy book.)[8]

However it cheers me to think that in poetry we have long thought of ourselves as starting not to start with the *logos* but the *pneuma*, not with those Platonic consonantal forms, but with the ether that encircles and unites them – the inspiration, the afflatus, the breath; the breath being the infinite possibility into which consonant, not vowel, must be driven to make it have any sense in the currency of our speech. This strikes me as a far more serious kind of word-game. Poets from Tennyson to Antonio Machado have

---

8. Kabbalistic exegesis is not quite as left-field as it sounds: some Semitic languages like Arabic and Hebrew work by using vowel-sounds to systematically modify a root group of consonants called a trilateral, or triconsonantal root. In Arabic 'k-t-b' is the 'write' group, and yields *kataba*, to write; *yaktubu*, he writes; *kitab*, book; *maktaba*, library, and so on. Hebrew does something very similar with the same trilateral. Pararhyme, if you like, is built into their structure: the Kabbalists and Sufis were really just imaginatively extending the rules of their own inflected morphology. English has no such excuses, and pararhymes generally sound a bit perverse if they're not concealed a little. Paul Muldoon does this beautifully through a mixture of wide separation and variable line-length; a uniform line would foreground them uncomfortably.

often lighted on 'wind' as the idealized inspirational source – shaping its one long vowel around every object it meets, embodying our paradoxical pursuit of unity through an utterly distinct articulation of the specific. And of course it brings weather, words, voices, scents from afar, from impossible elsewheres.

Singing works by 'unnaturally' elongating the vowel and so diminishing the prominence of the consonant. This can be seen in its treatment of end-rhymes; sung, the words *soon, room, cool, roof* are often perceived as close-to-full, and the longer the note, the closer they get. For lyricists, then, assonantal rhymes can work like full rhymes: when the Bobster sings "Let me sleep in your meadows with the green grassy leaves / Let me walk down the highway with my brother in peace", we're relatively untroubled by the inaccuracy of the rhyme, however upset some of us are by his voice. And as you'd expect, in exaggerating the vowel, singing will often foreground the emotional sense at the expense of the denotative.[9] Instrumental music itself may be considered usefully as an unbroken vowel, a kind of pure tonal and quantitative speech whose purpose is to carry emotion alone – like the spoken vowel, only vastly more supple and articulate. But the absence of consonant in music means that we are left with something possessive of emotional articulacy, but with no differentiating ability, no way to construct a sign-system, and thus no denotative power. When Richard Strauss said, with little irony: "I look forward to the day I can describe a teaspoon accurately in music," everyone was justifiably sceptical; indeed the teaspoon has remained wholly elusive as ever. In a good jazz ballad solo, especially in an instrument close in timbre to the voice, like a tenor saxophone, the displacement and pitch of the notes are so closely mapped to the rhythms and cadences of a plaintive and convincing conversational speech that you can easily imagine 'enconsonating' the notes to give a denotative sense. (Some 'vocalese' artists couldn't resist doing just that to a number of famous solos – with predictably farcical results.)[10] In a sense, however, poetry does precisely this: in making a normative shift towards privileging the vowel and so restoring some of the quantitative length found in speech, it edges

9. This is what people mean when they say things like "She could break your heart singing the phonebook". More practically, most librettists will have had the miserable experience of hearing their best line rendered unintelligible by having it set for long notes in the upper register of the soprano voice – which has the vowel /i/ and no other; though composers have devised a million other ways to lose lines too. This is one reason the librettist-composer relationship should sensibly be considered a co-operative, and not collaborative one.

10. Something to think about, or not: since consonant is the tool of differentiation, of denotative meaning, a block of consonant (like the Torah) seems to propose a monosemic source, which is why the multiple reinterpretations suggested by Kabbalistic re-envoweling appeared to many as wholly heretical; a block of vowel (like music), on the other hand, seems to imply a polysemic source, which is why a single interpretation seems *equally* heretical – as well as hilariously reductive, and instantly redundant. As anyone who has suffered Eddie Jefferson's enconsonation of Coleman Hawkins' classic solo on 'Body and Soul' will testify with alacrity. ("Don't you know he was the king of the saxophone," etc. No shit, man.)

towards a kind of transitive music.

It is this exaggerated prominence given to the vowel that primarily distinguishes the characteristic noise of the poem from prose or conversational speech, though the effect is very subtle. In received ideals of 'beautiful' English lyric, we tend to find, upon close examination of the texts, that vowels are strongly emphasized through a pattern of their deliberate contrast and variation, so that each word retains its distinct spirit, and has the sense of standing in a clearly-stated and discrete spatial and temporal relation to those on either side. (Or – a subject we have no space to cover here – through stark, consciously-perceived *deviation from that varied ground,* that is to say through assonance and rhyme. Assonance – think "That vase" from Larkin's 'Home is So Sad' – doesn't have any effect *unless* the changes are continually being rung elsewhere.) Varied vowels reinforce the impression that we are indeed saying things once, as the silence demands, with utter clarity. Try slowly mouthing just the vowel-sounds in the following passages (then compare them with a random chunk of journalistic prose as a 'control'):

> I caught a tremendous fish
> and held him beside the boat
> half out of water, with my hook
> fast in a corner of its mouth.
> > (Elizabeth Bishop, 'The Fish')

> 'This man can't bear our life here and will drown,'
> The abbot said, 'unless we help him.' So
> They did, the freed ship sailed, and the man climbed back
> Out of the marvellous as he had known it.
> > (Seamus Heaney, from 'Lightenings')

> I would spread the cloths under your feet:
> But I, being poor, have only my dreams;
> I have spread my dreams under your feet;
> Tread softly, because you tread on my dreams.
> > (W.B. Yeats, 'He Wishes for the Cloths of Heaven')

You should have felt like you were trying to deal with a gigantic and intractable toffee. Upping the 'fat' vowel count has the effect of lengthening the line, and is actively achieved by deliberate word-choice, and passively by lowering the occurrence of the thin ones. This means, essentially, keeping schwa down to a minimum. *Schwa* is the short neutral vowel sound that occurs in many unstressed syllables, and represented by the / ə / symbol in the

IPA. From the word for 'nought' in Hebrew, its nondescript micro-grunt can be substituted for any of the vowels, if they occur in an unstressed position: the 'a' in 'abet' and 'petal'; the 'e' in 'bagel'; the 'i' in stencil; the 'o' in 'arrogant' or 'condition'; the 'u' in 'crocus' and the 'y' in 'satyr', and so on. In rapid speech their numbers multiply. It can't be stressed or sustained, and it is no more possible to sing a long schwa than it is to play a two tied semibreves on the banjo.

One immediate consequence of writing in metre is that the unstressed syllable-count falls dramatically in comparison with a prose passage of equal length. Whatever other purposes it serves, metrical writing is also a great way of increasing the relative number of stressed syllables by insisting that every second syllable (in duple metres) or every third (in triple) are stressed. (This is a brutal oversimplification – this essay isn't about metre – but that's the principle.) This automatically lowers the schwa-count by making it harder for them to squeeze in. However, metred or not, the act of lineation *itself* serves to compel a slower spoken delivery, and this often results in the re-emergence of gobbled conversational schwas as fuller vowels. Poetry may indeed be 'chopped up prose' at times, but we use a magic knife. It allows silence to force its presence between the words, and for the breath within them to expand. Or, to relineate Bill Cosby:

> Always end
> the name
> of your child
> with a vowel
>
> so when
> you yell
> the name
> will carry.

Here, what would be schwa or near-schwa when spoken rapidly in a gag – 'always', 'your', 'so', 'you' and 'will' – move towards full vowels.

This vowel-promotion forms half the lyric ground. The effect is quiet and subtle, and the reader is wholly unconscious of its existence, but experiences it powerfully as sense of deepened length, space, breath, musicality and tonal (and hence emotional) differentiation. Now let's look at the other half: the consonants.

The use of consonants in the lyric ground is a fairly straightforward affair. If we employ the consonant as the tool of semantic differentiation, our project of unity will be broadly aided by our repeating them: this is, in effect, a global application of the phonosemantic principle covered in the first part of this essay. Since consonants take up little space, their musical effect only really becomes audible through their repetition (or their unique deviation from a repetitive ground). What we tend to find, as we did with the variation of vowel-sound, is that in 'musical' writing that there are subtle patterns of consonantal echo. Here's an unsubtle one, just to get the hang of it:

> Glory be to God for dappled things
> For skies of couple-colour as a brinded cow;
> For rose-moles all in stipple upon trout that swim;
> Fresh-firecoal chestnut-falls; finches' wings;
> Landscape plotted and pieced-fold, fallow, and plough
> [...]   (Gerard Manley Hopkins, 'God's Glory')[11]

Spelling is irrelevant to the ear, and it's a huge advantage for a poet to learn to hear and recognise close phonetic relatives; for compositional purposes they can often be freely substituted for one another. I'll list them here:

The unvoiced and voiced plosives: p/b, t/d and k/g
the fricatives: f/v, t/th [θ/ð], s/z, sh/zh [ʃ/ʒ] and h
the affricates: ch/j [tʃ/ʒd]
the nasals: m/n/ng [m/n/ŋ]
the glides and the liquids (more properly, approximants): w/wh/y [w/ʍ/j] and l/r [l/ɹ]

Most of these pairs or groups are close enough to function as interchangeable allophones in one language or another, l and r in Japanese being the best known example. (This is just a very rough guide, and the relations are far more involved; b/v are also allophones in some languages, and Grimm's consonant shift shows that the Classical unvoiced p/ t/ k stops were close enough to morph into the Germanic unvoiced f /th / h.)

The practical method of achieving a unified consonantal music in our lines is the same as the method for everything else: be alive to the possibility each line itself suggests, in the initial stages of its composition. (This super-sensitivity to the weight and texture of words is a faculty that tends, I suspect, to get burned into the circuits in the age of lyric innocence, during one's early adventures in voice-finding – Pound claimed this occurs between the ages of seventeen and twenty-two – but it could surely be learned by

---

11. Hopkins is great, of course – but he also holds perennial appeal for the tone deaf, as even they cannot fail to hear his glorious racket. Many of Hopkins' effects are spectacular, but are some-times achieved at the expense of his quieter ones; he can walk an uncomfortable line between a baroque lyricism and a demented echolalia. Nonetheless no poet trains the apprentice ear better, and neither Seamus Heaney nor George Mackay Brown – to name two marvellously attuned poets – would have had the ears they have without him.

anyone prepared to cultivate the necessary obsession.) The 'given' line or phrase will often hint at a kind of consonantal signature; the search for 'what it is that we mean' is then conducted through that narrowed lyric channel, shifting from line to line like another twist of the kaleidoscope. Thus consonantally restricted, every two- or three-line passage will start to exhibit its own distinctive colour. (This, for most of us, is work done best by the instinct, but it's worth repeating: the instinct can be consciously trained.) Essentially, the insistence that all expression must be woven into the local consonantal fabric creates a low-level formal resistance, to which the direction and content of our sense-making must adapt. This way we end up saying something better than the thing we intended to. This somewhat tricky idea can be better understood if we look at a more salient and isolable lyric effect: rhyme. (It would take another essay to accommodate the subject of rhyme properly, so I'll confine myself to this single aspect for now.)

Rhyme is a point, contrastingly, of *high*-level formal resistance. If rhyme is employed in a poem, it has little compositional value for the poet if it does not present a problem, regardless of how it might improve the sound of the poem for the reader. This is because the search for a rhyme is not a search for a synonym ("Ok – what means 'birth' and ends with -*ump*?") but for a solution to a broader question. Because English is such a rhyme-poor tongue, the chances of us finding a word that both makes the sound *and* the sense that we're after are effectively nil. The trick is to turn a problem into an opportunity: we search for rhymes in the *expectation* that our intended sense will change, since it is actually *desirable* that it do so. We are involved in a process, not an operation, and the resistant problem of finding a natural rhyme enforces that process, guarantees that it will *take time*: time to find out what we think, and discover what we did not know – not merely write down what we already do. If rhyme is going to be used at all, it has to be the principal formal consideration. The process of hunting and finding rhyme-pairs often dictates a large part of the content, as well as the syntax which must prepare for their natural fall. Poems where the poet has *refused to negotiate*, to allow the vector of their intended sense to alter by one degree, are marked by unnatural and unconvincing rhymes, and unnatural or hyperbatonic syntax, where the words have tripped over each other to shove the right one at the end. 'Rhyme' is a verb, not a noun, for poets, and implies a dynamic fluidity of sense and content – both of which can be cheerfully determined, in part, by the hunt for the rhymes themselves. Yeats claimed that if it wasn't for rhyme, he would't know what the next line was going to be.

Consonantal patterning can be considered a more diffuse version of the same idea; and this lyric workflow, this dovetailing of sound and sense, is the humming engine of our heuristic method: sense-modification in pursuit of the truth. In terms of how such a natural consonantal patterning can be achieved – well, I'm not big on exercises, but here's an instructive one. Take a noun and a random qualifier with different sounds in them; list the consonantal sounds separately; then try to compose a long sentence of words based on their permutations, with a few connectives and articles thrown in.[12] Thus 'leaf mould' might produce something like: *O deaf fellow, / dead failed mode / of my dumb foal – / deal me the foam, / the old model / of the fall, the leaf mould, the flume / of my love's veal...* Instant Hopkins! Absolute rubbish of course, because the strictures are way too severe to admit much sensible possibility, but you get the idea. By allowing (as we would normally, and as I had instinctively started to do by the end) the unvoiced and voiced siblings of 't' for 'd', 'v' for 'f', the 'n' and 'ng' for 'm', and the liquid 'r' for 'l' – we win ourselves much more lyric latitude, and this allows us to write in an unforced, natural way, and dampen the mad music. This method of free anagrammatizing is, when used instinctively, maybe the most effective way of uniting the music. Later in the poem's composition, when we're so often left with blanks to fill in a line, it's a useful trick just to take your musical bearings from the words on either side of the gap, and see if that input alone will lead you to the word. This is, of course, putting absolute trust in the phonosemantic principle. What's strange is how often it works – even when, and perhaps especially when, the sense is quite different from that which you intended.

Here's a fine example of consonantal weaving, from Douglas Dunn's *Elegies*:

> [...] And fastened to a mourning blink
> brought there by melanoma's
> sun-coaxed horrific oncos,
> leaving me to guess at
> what mysteries you knew
> foretold by love or creatures. ('The Sundial')

Look at that terrible, stunning line "sun-coaxed horrific oncos". "Sun-coaxed" and "oncos" are almost phonetic anagrams, and the assonantal "o"s stand in shocking, stark relief against Dunn's lovely variable-vowel default. Here's another example of what the fully-attuned poetic ear can do:

> The road to the burn
> is pails, gossip, gray linen.

---

12. We should never forget the music of the little words in our musical calculations however; schwa or no schwa, they also serve.

> The road to the shore
> is salt and tar.
>
> We call the track to the peats
> the kestrel road.
>
> The road to the kirk
> is a road of silences.
> (George Mackay Brown, 'Roads')

The reader knows it sounds beautiful, but doesn't know why. Nor should they. We do: in the first couplet, we have a salient alliteration with 'gossip, gray', but also the play of the l/r liquids, the p/b stops, and the nasal n; in the second, the sibilants s and sh, the plosive dentals d/t, and the liquids l/r again; in the third, the hard k, the l/r pair and the d/t pair; and in the fourth, the lovely self-descriptive sibilant singularity of "silences", hushed even further in its plural. All this is virtuosic, and I don't doubt largely instinctive, but again – it's an instinct trained by much practice. Besides, our ear-training provides us with the tools to correct bad lines: we can now say *why* they sound bad, and often the diagnosis is simply that the consonants are too disparate, and the vowels wholly unconsidered. *The path to the stream / is buckets, conversation, dirty washing.* Pretty grim, huh. The bulk of poetry written sounds like this. It might even be imagistically striking and intelligently argued, but it still sounds like a bag of spanners falling down a refuse chute. But also note how, as predicted by our phonosemantic rule, the sense *itself* is dismantled by incoherent music.

Finally, note how the formation of lyric ground consists in finding variation in that which is most similar (the vowel) and repetition in that which is most varied (the consonant). A general motif running through out poetic practice is not just normative shift, but language quietly turning against its own conventional patterns.

Let me wind this part up by proposing an analogy: consonant is to vowel as noun is to verb. Consonant is bounded form, non-durational, atemporal, like the static object; vowel is spatially free, durational, temporal, like the dynamic process. Consonant divides as instant and boundary divide; vowel unites as space and time unite. Somewhere in the unconscious, the echoed consonants imply similarities of form – and singular arrangements of them, differences; varied vowels imply spatial and temporal separation, and echoed vowels, space-time parallels, proximity, and similarities of interior spirit.

I mentioned that there are rough conclusions that can be drawn about a poem's music from several feet away. Held at this distance, poems can reveal themselves as compositionally askew in another way, but it's more subtle: it involves a lack of balance between abstract and concrete language. Now – this is neither here nor there in a single poem, and one poet will often demonstrate a bias one way or the other (Bishop's language is generally more concrete than Hardy's, for example); but over several poems, an addiction to concrete expression can have rather grave musical consequences. The problem lies with the consonants.

The more concretized language becomes in English, the more stop-heavy and consonantal it becomes. The more abstract it becomes, the more stop-light, and the higher the incidence of passages formed of 'open ended' words, where one or both ends of the vowel's envelope will not be shaped by stops, but by another vowel, or a fricative, an affricate, a glide or liquid. This interrupts the breath far less than usual, and keeps the air flowing from one word to the next; it can give the sense of a single breath moving through the whole line. This is the result of, firstly, the heavy use of a small part of the English lexis – the Anglo-Saxon deictic word-base of articles, connectives, prepositions, interrogative and relative adverbs with all their *shs* and *whs* and *ths* and *ys* and *hs* and *ws* and *fs* – which necessarily forms the bulk of such passages; and secondly, the use of Anglo-Saxon and Norman abstractions, which – to a far less obvious degree, but nonetheless a significant one – show a stop-light bias: *life, weight, fulfil, hurt, thought, death, future, anger, high, less.* (Counterexamples abound, as ever, so it's important to reiterate that these are diagnosable tendencies, no more.)[13]

Airiness in abstract passages, and plosive weight in concrete, have iconic functions. They point to the existence of a kind of globally diffuse phonestheme, where light stops and air-flow equal insubstantiality, lightness, and abstraction, while heavy stops equal substantiality, weight, and the delineated borders of the physical object. By applying the law of phonosemantic reciprocity, we might also posit that the 'dereification' of concrete expression might be effected by a shift away from a stop-based music – and indeed we can see evidence of this in the fact that, in concrete nouns, a move towards physical insubstantiality is often signed by the passage of air: *shift, chiffon, sheer, fluff, feather, ether, veil, flower, thin, breath.*

Listen to the relatively breathy and plosive-light music of the following passages:

---

13. Abstract language only becomes stop-heavy when it gets Latinate; here the sense of our ratiocinative precision, of our clear comparison of abstract forms, is reinforced by the 'concretization' of the music.

And since the whole thing's imagined anyhow,
Imagine being Kevin. Which is he?
>   (Seamus Heaney, 'St Kevin and the Blackbird')

[…] waking at times in the night she found assurance
In his regular breathing but wondered whether
It was really worth it and where
The river had flowed away
And where were the white flowers.
>   (Louis MacNeice, 'Les Sylphides')

It would be hard to say what brought them there,
commerce or contemplation.
>   (Elizabeth Bishop, 'Large Bad Picture')

I'd like to get away from earth awhile
And then come back to it and begin over.
May no fate wilfully misunderstand me
And half grant what I wish and snatch me away
Not to return.
>   (Robert Frost, 'Birches')

These days such lines require a bit more bravery on our part than they used to. A quick dip into Tennyson's 'In Memoriam' serves to remind us of the way in which it was once standard poetic practice to locate the poem wholly in the realm of abstract argument, and dip into the concrete only for illustrative exempla, metaphor, and anecdotal evidence. As a result, for all its marvellous argumentative strength, 'In Memoriam' sounds light as a feather. Show-not-tell is merely the dumb warcry at the head of a more insidious development: the over-concretization of the poetic voice. It is a neurotic response to the feeling that no one is listening. We have – correctly – perceived a bored and dwindling audience, and have instituted a manic attempt to keep them awake through data-reward, through the brain-sweets of image and anecdote. To get the air flowing in our poems again, we require the bravery of showing ourselves to be engaged in thought while in the *act* of writing. This is controversial among those of our number – and there are a fair few – who would claim that the poem is no place for notions, and indeed succeed effortlessly in writing poetry blissfully free of them. "No ideas but in things" was bad enough; but the current advice to 'keep it concrete, keep it simple'[14], whatever its other faults, has been a musical disaster.

14. 'Simple' is often a call for syntax to be kept paratactic and straightforward. Well... tell that to Yeats and Shakespeare. It's the syntax that betrays the subtly and sophistication of the thought, and complexity needn't mean a lack of clarity, or anything like it. Readers, I think, are bored senseless with poem after poem full of expository paratactic syntax; it patronizes them, and all but accuses them of being unable to follow an argument. Up with hypotaxis!

Lines where the air flows freely are simple phonetic artefacts of *thinking aloud*. Poems are epiphanic documents, and show the writer in the progress of *making* their discoveries so that the reader can re-enact and re-live them, not merely feel their after-effects, or learn the poets' wise conclusions. The total absence of all language which indicates argument, reflection, interrogation, conditionality, consideration and equivocation is often a sign that the poem is being written after the event, out what the poet already knows; this is often identical to what the reader already knows. An increase in air-flow is often a sign that the poet has been deeply detained in the who, the where, the when, the which, the how and why of it all – and through this mouth-mouth resuscitation, the reader's imagination is revived, awakened, ready to share in the live surprise of the poet's own journey.

Meeting Inna Lisnianskaya

ELAINE FEINSTEIN

Inna Lisnianskaya, a poet in her late seventies, is one of the most significant voices to come out of Russia in the last few years. Not only is her subject matter unusual, she has a lyricism which, as her translator Daniel Weissbort puts it, seems to *transcend language*; a precision of feeling so intense that we can respond, even when the rich texture of the Russian is absent.

Lisnianskaya's recognition has come late in life. Born in Baku in 1928, she was neither one of the writers favoured by the Soviet State, nor one of those popular nonconformists whom Akhmatova once rudely described as "stage poets". Nevertheless, she won the praise of Joseph Brodsky. She was awarded the prestigious Solzhenitsyn Prize in 1999 and the Russian State Prize in 2000. Years earlier Akhmatova warned Solzhenitsyn, after his novel *One Day in the Life of Ivan Denisovitch* had been published in *Novy Mir*, that "It is very difficult to endure fame, especially late fame". Lisnianskaya wears her own very lightly. By the time she tasted success, her personality was already formed: laconic, witty, self-mocking. When a journalist from *Literaturnaya Gazeta* came to interview her, she dismissed all commiserating questions with a casual and entirely characteristic: "I have had my say".

She lives part of the year in the writers' village of Peredelkino – half an hour outside Moscow – in a dacha she once shared with her late husband, Semyon Lipkin, who was not only a remarkable poet but a man of notable courage. It was with Lipkin that Vasily Grossman was able to hide, when the manuscript of his great novel *Life and Fate* was taken away by the KGB; it was with Lipkin, too, that the only surviving manuscript of the novel was hidden on a peg behind coats, until it could be microfilmed and sent to America for publication. Since Lipkin's death, Lisnianskaya spends the winter months with her daughter Elena and her son in law Sergei Makarov in Jerusalem. In April 2007 I was able to visit her there, taken by the poet Yvonne Green, who is working on translations of Semyon Lipkin's poetry with a group of writers including Daniel Weissbort.

Yvonne and I were both attending a conference of writers – with very disparate political attitudes – and staying in a hotel which had once been a British hospital, just below Mount Zion. That April, Jerusalem was bitterly cold, and a freezing wind blew under my clothes whenever I went out on the streets. We went by taxi to the German Colony, a salubrious part of

Jerusalem, where Elena and Sergei rent a flat on the second floor of an apartment block. They welcomed us in with the whispered news that Lisnianskaya was not feeling well.

That afternoon, Lisnianskaya was sitting on an unmade bed, still in her nightdress, with a candlewick dressing gown, barely secured by a twisted belt and spotted with a pattern of navy-blue blobs; her grey hair thin and a little straggly. Her features, though, were strong. Many of Akhmatova's visitors record being received with a similar lack of embarrassment about dress and disarray. Lisnianskaya held a cigarette between long fingers, which were – surprisingly, given her general air of indifference to appearances – markedly well manicured. Once a journalist from *Literaturnaya Gazeta* had watched her sitting with a cigarette, and drawn a comparison between her appearance and that of Akhmatova in the celebrated aquamarine and yellow portrait painted by Natan Alterman. Lisnianskaya did not welcome the flattery. "I'm comfortable enough with myself," she said dismissively.

She seemed in-turned that afternoon, however; presumably preoccupied by whatever health problem she was confronting. Her skin was sallow, there was not much colour in her lips. Elena whispered to us that she was very worried about her mother's health, and patted her chest, though whether to indicate a problem with heart or lungs I was not certain. She explained that Inna had an appointment for tests at the hospital later that day, adding that her mother particularly distrusted doctors and had to be persuaded to put herself in their hands, convinced that since she was without money or influence she would not be treated properly. In fact there is a good health service in Jerusalem which demands neither.

Elena's flat is not large, but there are four rooms opening out of the main living room, and the walls are covered with paintings and books. It is the home of educated people, loving art and poetry. Many of the paintings, I discovered, were made by victims of the Holocaust, notably Friedl Dicker-Brandeis, who died in Auschwitz. Their fate, and indeed the whole Jewish past, has fascinated Elena and Sergei for many years as journalists and documentary film makers. Some of their projects, notably their work on the writing and art of Terezin (see pp.123-4 – Ed.), have been funded by the Simon Weisenthal Centre.

The family's relationship both to Israel and that Jewish inheritance is not, however, a straightforward one. Semyon Lipkin was fully Jewish, and so would have had a J in his Soviet passport in the place where nationality is indicated; and Inna remembers her Jewish father, an army doctor who was wounded and decorated in the Second World War, dreaming of gas ovens. In a poem written when it was far from easy to travel to Israel from the Soviet

Union, she wished him a fiddler to "play Israel's lament" since she doubted whether he would ever reach his 'Forbidden Land'. However, Inna herself was baptised by her nanny as a child, as Boris Pasternak claimed to be. Her mother, in any case, was a Russian Orthodox woman, and Inna identifies herself as a Christian. She seems not to separate the two faiths very sharply. Perhaps it is little more than a bureaucratic matter, but Sergei and Elena probably got their Russian exit visas on the strength of Inna's Jewish father, since Elena is not Lipkin's daughter but the child of Inna's first marriage.

From Lisnianskaya's poems I gather that, whatever else, the landscape of Israel enchants her: the glowing coral reef in Eilat, the unfamiliar shapes of tuna and other fish, the vegetation of Jerusalem which is so luxuriant in comparison to the blank snows of a Moscow winter. She calls Jerusalem her "magic potion". For her, Israel is Abraham's country with "a Springtime renewed by Christ". Not that she is sentimental about Israel's February warmth. A verse from a poem written a year after Lipkin's death concludes with the chilling words, "Israel. Warmth. Terror." Russian is her language, however, ineluctably; and it is for that reason, as much as her wish to escape from the hot Middle Eastern summers she returns to her dacha outside Moscow. In Jerusalem, she writes:

> Around me is only Hebrew –
> What can I make of its guttural stresses?

That afternoon, as Inna sat stolidly, I searched for questions that might rouse her, but I cannot remember now what triggered her first vivid response. "Without Lipkin my life is – " she shrugged to complete the sentence, that Eastern European shrug which can mean so many things, and here conveyed a sense of her own life as valueless. Meeting such a bleak failure of self-esteem in a woman who had lived with spirit through some of the darkest years of the century, I was the more determined to tell her how much I admire her poetry, particularly her late poems in which she writes fearlessly about the love between men and women whose bodies have aged. One of my favourite lyrics in *Far from Sodom*, a selection edited and translated by Daniel Weissbort, is 'Jealousy', which describes with affectionate mockery how a possessive man cannot bear other people to share the attention he wants from his wife. The story opens before the poem starts, with the man leaving their apartment in a temper:

> I look out the window at the retreating back.
> Your jealousy is both touching and comical.

> Can't you see I am old and scary, a witch,
> And apart from you no-one needs me at all?

As I struggle to convey my admiration for the subtle analysis of a relationship built on angry dependency, and my own reasons for treasuring her honesty, the first genuine smile lights her face. Her hand no longer clutches her dressing gown. She asks me which other poems I like, and as I tell her I realise that her seeming depression comes, as so often, not from neglect (her daughter clearly looks after her well) or even illness but a loss of her own sense of self. I remember other poems I have loved. And she speaks them in Russian for me; she has a deep cigarette-husky voice, not so unlike the voice of Akhmatova on the famous Gleb Struve recording made in Paris towards the end of her life.

Joseph Brodsky has already observed that Akhmatova's is the voice from the Russian past he can most readily sense in Lisnianskaya's poetry. Certainly, the literal, bony directness resembles hers; but Lisnianskaya is far readier to expose her own indignities. After the collapse of Communism, when she and her husband were first able to visit Jerusalem, she wrote a poem which involved a pitiless scrutiny of aging flesh:

> I'm your Shulamith, my old King Solomon,
> Your muscles are slack, but your sight still sharp.
> Nothing's withheld from you, but peering at the slope,
> You do not recognise me, draped from head to foot
> Among the women gathering grapes.

She confesses ruefully that her husband would know her no better if she were naked, even if she revealed her "belly / like undulant sands, legs stiff, unlike vine / My breast, the withered fruit from an ancient palm." Fortunately, their love for one another had always been fed by an exchange of songs – she remembers particularly the loving words he found to compare her hair to flashing sunlight – and so even in old age she can rejoice in him:

> I inhaled your speech, as a bee inhales pollen,
> My king, Solomon, your love hymn to beauty.

As I fumbled to express my admiration, with the help of Elena whose English is excellent, her face changed utterly. I suddenly understood how that interviewer from *Literaturnaya Gazeta* had come to compare her beauty to that of Akhmatova. In fact, there is little facial resemblance; Akhmatova's face was a pure oval to the end of her days, her lips narrow and tender; Lisnianskaya face is at once broader and flatter. But there us the same ironic poise, the same calm spirit, the same inner strength.

As I was thinking as much, the telephone rang and Elena came to tell Inna that the hospital had postponed the appointment. She seemed delighted. And suddenly she was bounding off the bed, and had taken her place at the kitchen table. Her daughter made tea. I could have been in any number of the houses I had visited in Russia. Inna had recovered an appetite, and it seemed credible that she had indeed, on another occasion, enjoyed being taken out to eat in a good restaurant by Yvonne. While her mother ate, Elena explained her own political position, which was somewhat to the left of Inna's, she hinted. Lisnianakya looked happy to allow her to take the centre stage: there is an unusual affection between mother and daughter.

Soon we were all drinking a splendid Estonian vodka.

Elaine Feinstein's most recent book of poetry is *Talking to the Dead* (Carcanet, 2007). Her biography of Anna Akhmotiva is *Anna of All the Russias* (Phoenix, 2006).

NB The translations used here are by Daniel Weissbort; more of his translations of Lisnianskaya appear on pp.16-19.

Kitchen Metaphysics:
An Interview With Charles Simic

DONOVAN MCABEE

One thing that struck me about your poetry when I first started reading it is an underlying assumption that existence is a good thing. Sometimes it comes out in exuberance, when you're talking about sex or onions, and in the darker poems there's still, if not an affirmation of life, then at least a resignation to live.

CS: Well, I think that's true, absolutely true. I'm sort of philosophically a pessimist. I don't think human beings are going to improve. People are the same nasty, small-minded, petty fools they've always been. As far as affirmation goes, yes, walking into a flower garden on a sunny day is wonderful. I have no complaints about that. So, I'm a cheerful pessimist.

You talk early in your career about looking for a "mythic consciousness" or for "the roots of our local imagination". Later, you say that you've quit looking for an American mythic consciousness. In reading your work, though, I don't believe you on this point.

CS: I used to be very much interested in myth, and I did a lot of reading in folklore and was interested in Native American lore, but especially regional traditions, superstitions, tall tales, beliefs. I would discover things that sound like pure surrealism, crazy stuff, like "counting sunbeams in a cucumber", and I thought that I would eventually discover its philosophical underpinnings, the way native poetic consciousness works, an outlook on life reflected in this stuff.

Being in New England, I read a lot about this region, but I gave it up when I realized it was becoming more of an intellectual project than something that I believed in. I mean, all I really wanted was a licence to use my imagination with the same kind of freedom. I wasn't going to spend my life sorting out what of that material was authentically native and what was brought over from England or some other place. I lost interest in that kind of speculation.

That was the period when you were writing pared-down poems...

CS: Yep.

The object poems. But it seems, to me at least, you let that sort of ribald sense of life in, where you have magical fat women outside of trailers, poems like 'Euclid Avenue', 'Avenue of the Americas'. These poems seem to demonstrate what you mean when you say that the only way to write poems now is in a style that encompasses a couple hundred channels of cable television with TV preachers at two in the morning. Maybe you wouldn't use the term "mythic consciousness", but it seems to me this is the American consciousness.

CS: It *is* American. Variety, contradictions, the sheer lunacy of it all, that's what Cable TV is. Now it's been cleaned up a lot but at first, when it came out, that kind of TV was exhilarating. I remember being stuck in a motel in those years, surfing the channels for hours. It just took my breath away: hardcore porn next to a Catholic channel where a nun is fingering her rosaries and praying. Some people get upset by things like that. They see that and say, "Aww, God, we are going to hell". I love it. There's some sort of vitality. The more the better. What makes this country great is that nothing makes sense. Contradictions. Many, many of them, like in that poem 'Avenue of the Americas' or the one about the fat woman in her trailer watching President Bush on TV. It's not that I make any of it up. I just see something like that and say to myself, "wonderful".

Everyone tries to put a name on whatever it is you're writing. You've been called a neo-surrealist, a neo-imagist. I even found one place where you are referred to as a Confessional poet, which I thought was a joke. What about your poems evades these labels?

CS: I think it's because I do many different things. I'm perfectly happy to have poems that seem dream-like or have images that one associates with surrealism. On the other hand, I'm also a hard-nosed realist, totally aware of what goes on around me. I report what I see both with my eyes open and with my eyes closed. I don't have a commitment to one aesthetic view or position. It all depends on my mood, or rather on the nature of the experience.

I'm not really a Confessional poet either. They are liars too. It's a strategy, to sound sincere, to sound like I'm telling you everything about myself. "I almost killed my mother once." The reader says, "Really?" "I pointed a gun…" "And what?" But even that's just bullshit. I'm much more interested in making a poem, and if I have to change things to make a better poem, then I will lie, steal. I don't care what happened to me. I never had much of an allegiance to being sincere or true to myself. Sincerity is not an aesthetic category.

Labelling is what reviewers usually do. It all started when I was publishing in *Kayak*, a surrealist magazine. George Hitchcock, the editor, was interested in poets who used images in wild and unpredictable ways in poems that sounded like they were written by people who had a few screws loose. The critics assumed we were imitating the French, Spanish and South American poets. We *were* a little, but it wasn't our main interest. I knew when I was eighteen years old that surrealism was old hat, but it was lots of fun to read. It allowed you to do certain things when it came to images, similes and metaphors. You could be more inventive, more wild. Still, if you read someone like James Tate, you realized his surrealism was native. Kansas, where he grew up, also produced Buster Keaton, another artist whose zaniness is strictly American. In any case, the label stuck. The implication was that our poems were meaningless. We were a bunch of wankers not to be taken seriously. I don't know about the others, but I have never been interested in poems that don't mean anything. I have difficulty reading Ashbery for that very reason – wonderful stuff, but it's hard to get a sense of what is really happening in his poems. I like Whitman, Dickinson, Frost and Stevens too. They take an experience, something in the world or something in their head, and then look at it very closely, examine it, and the poem tells us about it so that by the time we get to the end we have some idea why all this matters. As poets, we owe that much to the reader.

There often seems to be a charged feeling to your poems. The characters and places feel almost emblematic, symbolic even.

CS: I have always liked the Symbolists, not their cultivation of the 'poetic' and their hermeticism, but their way of turning an image in a poem into a symbol around which ideas begin to swarm. In other words, I don't drag some already established symbol or a myth into a poem but discover it right there. I do that by beginning to understand what kind of meanings some image is carrying.

It collects meanings along the way.

CS: Yes.

Flannery O'Connor talks in an essay about how the main character's car in Wise Blood *began to take on meaning as she wrote. I think she said as she wrote, it became a death-in-life symbol, this shitty old car.*

CS: I believe that. That's my ideal too. The jalopy – a poem is like that. Plop, plop, plop.

In one of your essays, you ask the rhetorical question, "How many literary theorists and teachers of literature truly understand that poems are not written namely for the sake of oneself, or for the sake of some idea, or for the sake of the reader but out of a deep and noble reverence for the old and noble art of poetry?" At what point did that sink in for you? It's not really there at the impulse.

CS: No, it's not. When you start writing, you don't know exactly why you're writing. Somebody's writing, a friend is writing, and you want to. But later on, I realized what keeps me going is memory of the poems I love and would have given everything, you know, my life, to have written. I don't want to write the same poems, but they give me a sense of standard. I want something so full, so powerful, but I don't want to do the same thing, so that creates problems. I have to find my own way.

It seems to me that British poets almost naturally have a sense of working within a tradition, a weight of tradition that they de facto *carry with them.*

CS: I agree.

And when you're an American poet, it's almost like you're still writing out into the darkness.

CS: Yeah, you have to find your own tradition. You shop around. You try this, you try that. You say, "I'm not gonna be Robinson Jeffers. I'm not gonna be John Crow Ransom". Then, you go and figure out what you're gonna be. But even then, when you find some place where you belong, you don't feel the weight of a tradition in the way they do. I'm very comfortable in New England, because I like this area and I know a lot about it, and I like living here, but I don't feel that strong a connection with Dickinson and Frost since I've lived in other places and loved poets who have nothing to do with this region.

Our tradition, most would say, only goes back as far as Whitman, Poe, and Dickinson. So, a distinctly 'American' poetic tradition is not very old. In addition to this, there's a certain eclecticism built into the genetic code of American poetry. Do you think those are factors that affect American poets who are trying to figure out where they belong?

CS: I do believe those are factors. Nowadays, for anyone writing in America there are so many competing traditions and identities to undermine whatever sense of self and belonging one has started with. If we have a tradition in poetry – and we do – it goes back to the Transcendentalists and their empirical approach to experience, the whole idea that you begin with something concrete and then take it from there wherever it leads to. What W.C.Williams called "no ideas but in things". What is always astonishing to foreigners who read American poetry is just that, the insistence on the part of the poet that *this really happened to me*. Like Elizabeth Bishop beginning a poem by saying, "I caught a tremendous fish" and then describing in minute details what she saw and what was in her mind as she pulled the fish out of water. That really is ours. We like it. But it's unpoetic too. I can't think of any European poet who writes like that, but we can't get enough of that kind of stuff. We are always worrying about our readers not believing our poems. So, we pretend that everything happened just as we say it did.

The place of the individual, it has a different status in American poetry.

CS: Well, it's all we trust. We trust the individual to make sense of things, to discover his own truths, even when it comes to God.

It's very Emersonian.

CS: Yes. You have Stevens's "no ideas about things but the thing itself", or something like that, a variation on that theme. But it always has to begin with the concrete. Don't begin by saying, "my soul". Describe your feet, your toes, the shoes you wear, instead. Every abstract notion is suspect until it has been tested through experience.

Your sense of the self was formed while being shuffled around by totalitarian governments, and you ended up in this country, with its tradition of mistrusting institutions and its ultimate trust in individuals. It seems to me that your personal history taps into this stream of American individualism.

CS: You are right. America was a good place for me to end up with all my historical experience. It was healing. Here – at least till now – they have left the individual alone. You didn't have to jump up and shout for hours how much you love the Republican Party or the Democrats. You could badmouth the President and the politicians to your heart's content. That's what I like about Emily Dickinson. She wanted to preserve her independence too.

There are forms of individualism that are oppressive – for instance, trying to recast the other in one's own image – but your narrators are different. You talk about how you want the 'I' of the reader to step into the 'I' of the narrator. That space happens in your poems. The form of individualism that comes through in your poetry creates a sense of space.

CS: For me, a poem is a place where one invites someone in. You build a little house, fix it all up real nice. Inside, you've got some interesting things you want to show them. You've got a painting on the wall, a new couch, some knick-knacks and souvenirs, a swell meal all laid out on the table, and you open the door and hope somebody comes in. The really wonderful thing about certain poems is, you start reading them, and find yourself after three or four lines inside somebody's head and somebody's reality. You had no idea before where you were going to be, but suddenly there you are and you like being there. That's what keeps me from dwelling too much on myself in a poem. I'm always more worried about this unknown other who's going to come in. They've got to come in because without them there is no poem. A poem is a collaboration between the reader and the poet.

That's a really interesting idea, the way a reader comes into a poem. I guess you give them the raw material for the experience, or even more than the raw material…

CS: They close the book, but they can't forget where they've been. It haunts them.

They think about some chair, the cracks on the ceiling, the way the night fell as they stood looking out of the window at the street below. They know there's more to it. We've got them trapped.

Inciting them to think.

CS: To feel too.

"Poetic thinking" as you talk about it, entails following the poem out to whatever it wants to be. This is itself a way of interrogating. In this process what is it that poems are trying to do? Are they trying to recognize reality? Are they trying to create a new reality? How do the poems relate to our thinking?

CS: In a poem we are always doing the impossible. Reality is always in the past, and yet we want it in the poem. Language, however, cannot grasp the immediate. As soon as we open our mouth, it's no more. Been here and gone. I want the light that fell in my bedroom when I was eleven years old on a particular Sunday morning, just as it was then. I want the vividness of the original experience. It can't be done, and yet it happens. Poems do that despite the seemingly infinite odds.

Poetry is a sort of kitchen metaphysics – or is it theology? Poets worry about God, worry about the self, being and nothingness, and what-have-you, but unlike philosophers and priests, they do not think of them apart from the ordinary reality of our lives. It's all somehow connected. There's a woman, she's annoyed with her children, annoyed with her husband. She starts peeling the potatoes; she cuts her finger; she throws the damn potato across the kitchen, hits the cat. If the so-called ultimate questions cannot be found right here in the dust of her floor, as it were, they're a lie. In my poetry sacred and profane sleep in the same bed, the angels are illegal aliens washing dishes in a restaurant, the philosopher Heraclitus takes his dog for a walk and in a burst of inspiration buys him a tennis ball. What I like about poetry is that it is not afraid to mix it all up.

I guess it shouldn't surprise us that the poets who talk most about the inability of words to communicate reality are the ones who often communicate the very least in their poetry.

CS: I think that's very well put. I just reviewed a book by the French poet Yves Bonnefoy. His main idea is that language fails to convey being. So, his poetry is constantly about this inability, this impotence to do that. I got a little tired of that. What he is saying is both true and not true. If you read Whitman's 'Crossing Brooklyn Ferry', at some point you really feel you are there, standing right next to Walt, leaning over the rails, looking at the sky and the waters, the towers of Manhattan as they're approaching. What people like Bonnefoy leave out is imagination. Yes, we know words can't say that, but that's not the only faculty we have, the language. There's also our imagination which can take a hint from the words and bring a whole world to life.

The notebook form that you often write in resembles a mediaeval miscellany.

CS: I suppose so. Whenever something pops into my head, or I see something or read something, I write it down and usually forget all about it. Sometimes the scribbling leads to more scribbling. In other words, I find myself interested and playing with words. These are not aphorisms, epigrams, or a journal, just a miscellany, as you say, odds and ends without rhyme or reason.

You say that in the twentieth century, humour became ontological, and I'm wondering why it took so long.

CS: Well, you could get in trouble for saying that. Humour was always an unofficial, irreverent view of reality. There is a strange notion almost everywhere that tragedy is a higher form of art than comedy, and yet neither I nor anyone else, I imagine, has meet anyone who resembles the characters in Greek tragedies. As for Aristophanes and other comic writers, these types are still around. It is with comedy that realism comes into literature. It tells how schmucks like me live, what they do, how they bicker and fight, cheat on their wives, make fools of themselves as cheating husbands, professors, generals and clergymen. Byron was pretty funny, but something happened in the nineteenth century, humour became light verse. It always seemed to me that laughter is as much a part of our experience as grief. We laugh even at funerals while trying not to. So, for humour not to be part of poetry, it's ridiculous.

How did you get permission to be funny in poetry?

CS: I guess it starts when you begin to make fun of poems and poetry. Jim Tate and I once wrote a poem where we tried to imitate Baudelaire. We took out some of his vocabulary, words like *azure, hashish, black cat*, etc. and tried to exaggerate the effect. I think some of that kind of horsing around gave us the idea. There were other influences as well. The American poet Kenneth Koch is funny. Frank O'Hara is also funny. A Chilean poet, whose work was translated in the late 60's and early 70's, Nicanor Parra, was an influence. His poems are hilarious. Russell Edson, who started writing those prose poems in the mid-50s is another gagster. He'd give poetry readings where people would roll in the aisles. I went to a reading in New York, where James Tate, Russell Edson, and Bill Knott read. People screamed, loved it. We were walking out, when I overheard a couple of women ahead of me talking. One said to the other, "Wasn't that great?" The other said, "Sure was, but you know, that's not poetry" .

You've always interacted with religious thinkers in your poetry: John of the Cross, Julian of Norwich, Thomas Aquinas. But it seems that in your last few collections, you deal with religious issues more directly.

CS: It's in my blood, as it were. Until my grandfather on my mother's side, who was a military man, they were all priests for a couple of centuries. I've always had immense interest in religion, religions; I've read everything, east and west and so forth. I'm Eastern Orthodox, Serbian Orthodox. My own beliefs are complicated, depending on what day you ask me. Tuesday I may be a believer. Wednesday a blasphemer. It always seemed to me that religious life, religious ideas are at the heart of our existence. You can't avoid God. I have an old friend in New York who shocked me one day. We were talking just like we're talking now, and he said to me, "You know, Charles, when you come to think of it, every poem is addressed to God". I was surprised, but when I thought about it, it made sense. Whether God exists or not, any serious poem comes around to him sooner or later. If he keeps coming back in my poetry, it's because there are a lot of things that I haven't resolved. Some guy from Georgia once sent me a Bible. I really appreciate that. He read my poems and understood that I was a sinner. I wrote him a nice letter. I said thank you very much. I still have the Bible today.

Did he tell you which sections to pay attention to?

CS: No, he didn't. There was no note.

Just the Bible?

CS: Yeah.

5 January 2007
Durham, New Hampshire

REVIEWS

ↆↆ

Really, a poetry without abstraction is just as
impoverished as a poetry without specifics.
—*Danielle Chapman*

Seeing Things Straight

JON COOK

C.K. Williams, *Collected Poems*, Bloodaxe, £20, ISBN 1852247533

Is there a signature C. K. Williams poem? Readers familiar with his work might think of it as something like this: a poem that begins in attentive observation or recollection of some everyday scene – a woman on a subway, for example, or a child playing in a park – which develops through an elaborate syntax into something like a revelation or a perplexity; a particular sense that the world's appearances can absorb our attention at the same time as they hint at something more, something undisclosed that might be menacing or benign. It is as though most of the time we live in a cloud of unknowing, or some state of illusion or denial; and the poem's purpose is not exactly to shock us out of this state but lead us to some point of acknowledgement. A woman on the subway turns out to have an artificial hand. Williams's poem is about how this oddity is denied and then admitted, almost by accident, and then how the woman herself acknowledges her own oddity, and looks at her hand "the way someone would glance at their unruly, apparently ferocious but really quite friendly dog".

Few poets have written about the curious, unbidden intimacies and submerged rituals of modern life with such insight. This particular poem is called 'Hooks' and it comes from Williams's 1987 collection, *Flesh and Blood*. There are many others that carry the same quiet authority; a telling of how it is, of how oddity of one sort or another is not something exceptional but the common currency of what we are to ourselves and to one another.

In a prose piece, published in 1983, 'Contexts: an Essay on Intentions', Williams wrote that poetry's purpose is "to offer evidence". "We have to know what is there before us, we have to have the facts, and to get them straight[...]." This identifies at least one half of his distinctive poetics and points to one kind of rationale for the long lines that are often, and sometimes mistakenly, thought of as another aspect of Williams's signature. There is so much there before us, and so much to get straight, that an elaborated line is needed not so much to *contain* these activities of seeing and getting things straight as to *sustain* them.

To say this is to say something obvious but important. Williams is a poet of consciousness. He inherits the Romantic and Modernist preoccupation with the poem as an act of mind. But the mind's action in a Williams poem is complex: muddied, full of fear and grief and guilt as well as the possibilities of redemption or, at least, repair. The scope and sprawl of these poems have led understandably to comparisons with Whitman. Both are great poets of democratic awareness. Both delight in the disorder of democracy as well as in its promise of a new egalitarian sociability. But Williams is a poet chastened by history. The first poem in this volume, 'A Day for Anne Frank', defines an important subject for Williams or, more accurately, a searching question. Consciousness may be the source of fine discriminations or a delicate exploration of our awareness of the world. It has also been the source of a terrifying obliviousness and violence. 'A Day for Anne Frank' moves abruptly between intimations of a terrible will to violence and degradation that produced the Holocaust and the impossible imaginative effort to rescue or redeem one of its victims. Repairing things – roofs, engines, bits of fabric – is one of Williams's recurrent subjects. It is also a metaphor for the kinds of things that a poem can do, and it is not surprising that the word "repair" gives the title to the collection that won the Pulitzer Prize in 1999. But the enduring, tenacious action of making something good again has its own limits and ambiguities. If the past in Williams's poetry is haunted by irreparable actions like the Holocaust, the future is charged with the prospect of environmental catastrophe. The margins of consolation and hope that Williams's poetry consistently works toward are, equally consistently, under threat.

The *Collected Poems* brings together in one book the work of nearly forty years. What it tells us is that, despite sceptical reservations to the contrary, poetry can still be a major art. Few poets working in English have Williams's technical inventiveness. He has brought the resources of prose forms like the essay, the anecdote and the short story into poetry. Few poets have his linguistic range moving from demotic informal utterance to lines of airy, Latinate elegance. This is a publication to be celebrated. More importantly, it's a book to be read and re-read.

Jon Cook is Professor of English, and Director of the Centre for Creative and Performing Arts, at the University of East Anglia.

Almost Done

MARK FORD

Elizabeth Bishop ed. Alice Quinn, *Edgar Allan Poe & the Juke-Box:
Uncollected Poems, Drafts, and Fragments*, Carcanet, £16.95,
ISBN 9781857549010

'**D**o / you still,' Robert Lowell asked in the last of his sonnets for
Elizabeth Bishop,

> hang your words in air ten years
> unfinished, glued to your notice board, with gaps
> or empties for the unimaginable phrase –
> unerring Muse who makes the casual perfect?

Until the publication of this volume, only those Bishop scholars who had
sifted through the archive of her papers held at Vassar had a full
understanding of the kinds of labour involved in perfecting the casual.
Bishop herself likened the processes of composition to fashioning an
imitation eye; and over the years worked, alas unsuccessfully, on a poem that
would have developed this analogy fully. For this most fastidious of writers
a poem that works must be at once "as normal as sight and yet as synthetic,
as artificial, as a glass eye."

Bishop would probably have been horrified to see these drafts and
fragments, abandoned in mid-synthesis, enshrined in print and picked-over
in endnotes that often stretch over many pages. The material assembled here
is in various ways fascinating, revealing, and moving, but couldn't be said to
contain any secret masterpieces that should immediately be added to the
Bishop canon. In a way this is reassuring: Bishop knew what she was about.
One reads these poems with a mixture of regret and frustration that so
many potentially wonderful poems never came into being, but also with an
enhanced feeling of gratitude for those that did.

Bishop's poems evolved in the manner laid out in Lowell's sonnet; she
didn't get the first line right, then the next, then the next, but developed a
kind of skeleton of the poem, which successive drafts would flesh out. A
particular concept lurks behind many Bishop poems, though the gap
between the idea and its poetic completion could be many decades. On a
trip to Cuttyhunk Island in the summer of 1934, for instance, she observed

in her notebook that on an island one lives like Robinson Crusoe, "contriving and inventing", and that "a poem should be made about making things in a pinch – and how it looks sad when the emergency is over." Thirty-five years would elapse before 'Crusoe in England', the poem based on this idea, saw the light of day.

Many of the proto-poems collected here are based on ideas as enticing and potentially rewarding as those that resulted in pieces that the poet did manage to finish. It is not really possible to determine what prevented this or that draft ever getting air-borne; to work out, why, for instance, Bishop was unable to get far with poems on such quintessentially Bishopian subjects as her beloved toucan, Uncle Sammy, whom she inadvertently poisoned when treating him for fleas, or the canaries, Dicky and Sister, kept by her Aunt Maud in the house in Revere where Bishop lived between the ages of seven and sixteen. She struggled on and off with these bird poems for many years, and claimed the Sammy one was almost complete, though the fragments presented here suggest much remained to be done.

It is tempting to see attempts at more personal topics, such as her alcoholism, her lesbianism, or the suicide of her partner of fifteen years, the Brazilian Lota de Macedo Soares, as inevitably doomed. Bishop abhorred the 60s rage for Confessional poetry, and 'The Drunkard' and 'Vague Poem' must have struck her as veering far too close to self-revelation. The latter culminates in her most explicit celebration of the joys of sex:

> Just now, when I saw you naked again,
> I thought the same words: rose-rock, rock-rose...
> Rose, trying, working, to show itself
> forming, folding over,
> unimaginable connections, unseen shining edges.
> Rose-rock, unformed, flesh beginning, crystal by crystal,
> clear pink breasts and darker, crystalline nipples...

It is a particular shame that her planned elegy for Lota, with its haunting refrain, "No coffee can wake you no coffee can wake you no coffee can wake you," survives only in the sketchiest of drafts, though at one point she envisaged it as a book-length poem, and applied for a Guggenheim Fellowship to work on it as late as 1977, two years before her own death.

The most nearly finished poem in the book, and the one that is closest to being a genuine addition to the *Complete Poems*, is the last, 'Mr and Mrs Carlyle'. This was probably begun in the early sixties; in a letter of July 1978 to Frank Bidart she reports it "almost done", and its five quatrain stanzas are nicely polished and more or less ready to go. The poem is an attempt to capture the famously tempestuous relationship between Thomas and Jane Carlyle by describing a failed rendezvous at a pub called The Swan with Two Necks. Its brilliant final stanza achieves the delicately poised balance between comedy and pain that characterizes so much of Bishop's finest writing:

> One flesh and two heads
>   engaged in kisses or in pecks
> Oh white seething marriage!
>   Oh Swan with Two Necks!

Mark Ford's collections of poetry are *Landlocked* and *Soft Soft*. His volume of essays is *A Driftwood Altar*.

Portents of Crises

JAMIE MCKENDRICK

Poems of Georg Trakl, trans. Margitt Lehbert, Anvil, £9.95, ISBN 9780856462856; *Poems of Paul Celan*, trans. Michael Hamburger, Anvil, £19.95, ISBN 0856462659; Paul Celan, *Snow Part / Schneepart*, trans. Ian Fairley, Carcanet, £14.95, ISBN 9781857549447; D.M.Black, *Love as Landscape Painter, Translations from Johann Wolfgang von Goethe*, Fras Publications (The Atholl Browse Bookshop, Blair Atholl), £8.50, ISBN 9781857549447

Anyone who translates poems will be aware of a kind of Zeno's paradox by which the nearer the text approximates to the original the further away it becomes. And nowhere can this law of diminishing returns be more keenly felt than with the German poets Paul Celan and Georg Trakl. Trakl would seem the easier of the two. Surely English could manage something like the weird and pregnant stillness of his lines – with their air of a curdled idyll? Yet without Trakl's music, his tone and sonority, translation falls into bathos and Gothic stage-props.

Berryman summed up Trakl's short, blighted career in a one-line title:

'Drugs Alcohol Little Sister' – and his life indeed seems to have spun ever further from a stable axis until his breakdown in 1914, in Grödek where he was working as a military nurse, and his suicide in Cracow soon after from a cocaine overdose. There's a troubling sense, though, in which the personal catastrophe of Trakl's life figures, at least in the poems, as a portent of a larger, European crisis – cultural unease, loss of religious faith, an encroaching decay – which will come to a head in the First World War.

Lehbert's translations include all of the poems of Trakl's two books and the late poems he didn't live to publish. It's a shame that her understanding of the originals is unmatched by her performance in English – too often her lines lack tension and music, are enervated or fall back into trite, sub-Tennysonian inversions: "Over parkland grieved and pale / [...] In putrescence sweet and stale [...]". In 'Melancholy in Evening', the over-dubitative line "And maybe stars, perhaps, are also shining" is just not feasible in English. (The original is not so doubtful and gains force from its alliteration.) In her version of Trakl's extraordinary early poem 'The Rats' we read: "And a horrid haze of something foul / Wafts after them from the toilet / That ghostly moonlight shudders through [...]". Compare Robert Grenier's version of these lines in the long-extinct *Selected Poems* (Cape): "A greyish dust-haze reeks / After them from the latrine, through which / The spectral moonlight shivers." Flat as this is, there's at least a hint of something uncanny; and even though Lehbert's volume is far more inclusive, I would still recommend that slender, bi-lingual edition, translated by several hands (including Michael Hamburger), for those who want some idea of what makes Trakl such a haunting and singular poet.

Celan's poems are if anything even less susceptible to translation. Born in Bukovina in 1920, Celan escaped when Germany invaded but both his parents died in a concentration camp, his father of typhoid, his mother shot. This violence and the evil of those years mark everything he wrote until his suicide in 1970. The poet and translator Michael Hamburger, who died earlier this year, has toiled for several decades gradually adding to his translations of Celan. This now-posthumous volume is the sum of that exacting and exhausting work. The results are uneven; although I'm not sure how they could ever be otherwise. Best in English, it seems to me, are the poems from the first book. Their songlike rhythms (often amphibrachs as in "*Du füllst hier die Urnen und speisest dein Herz*" – "You fill up the urns here and nourish your heart") which Hamburger skilfully reproduces, and their uncanny juxtapositions, reach a crescendo in his famous 'Death Fugue'. Thereafter Celan chooses to break up the surfaces of his poems, to create a language which turns in on itself, examining with the utmost scrupulousness its own formations, its cognates, its parts of speech, as if only in language was there any refuge, and even that refuge has to be secured with infinite care. In the beautiful version here of Celan's poem to Mandelstam "things lost were things not lost, / the heart was a place made fast." The poems turn inward, resist entry, and Celan freights every utterance with almost more weight and meaning than words can bear.

His difficulty, as he himself argued and as Hamburger repeats, is not hermeticism. Unlike some forms of experimental writing which might claim Celan as a precursor, his difficulty proceeds from a surfeit not a paucity of meaning. You can see why, consummate as it is, the poet repudiated 'Death Fugue' in his unwillingness to find "solace in euphony" (Trakl's phrase).

These difficulties multiply with translation. In Celan's much-commentated yet still elusive 'Todtnauberg', which records a visit to Heidegger's forest retreat, medicinal flowers – arnica, eyebright – stand like hopeful witnesses at the threshold of the poem. "Whose name" Celan wonders, precedes his own in the visitors' book? Celan's hope of some "word in the heart" that will confront or revoke the philosopher's enthusiastic support of Nazi Germany proves unfounded. The poem ends: "*die halb- / beschrittenen Knüppel- / pfade in Hochmoor, // Feuchtes, / viel*". Hamburger: "the half- /trodden fascine /walks over the high moors, // dampness, / much." The word "fascine" – meaning a brushwood faggot – with its sinister reprisal of "fasces" is an ingenious solution but too recherché. The word lacks the consonantal, physical immediacy of "*Knüppel*" (a stick – perhaps to beat someone with). It's an example of how in Celan, whilst the meaning is elusive, the German remains palpable; and of how, especially when it moves towards the Latinate, English can lose purchase on his poems.

Ian Fairley has translated *Schneepart* (1970) with Celan's late poems. Like Hamburger's accompanying essays, Fairley's introduction brilliantly illuminates many aspects of Celan's work, the intricacies of his language, as well as the challenge of translating him. His own versions defy my initial proposition: they adhere as closely as they can to the German, diction and compounds, and unearth a living stratum of German in English, translating, for example, "*setz Lee über Luv*" as "sets lee over luff". This can lead him into barely construable lines like "strewing things timeunderhallowed" or to a phonetically nonsensical enjambment such as "the sack of mutter- / ed resolutions" (presumably here to register the un-enjambed compound "*Beschlußmurmeln*") but these are risks he seems willing to take. Where Hamburger, more conservatively, tends to respect what is possible in English, Fairley tries to extend that possibility. Any English reader of Celan owes a debt of gratitude to both translators. Even if so much eludes English in both, enough gets through to leave a sure sense that the loss and tenderness which resound through Celan's poems are like nothing else on earth.

To read D.M.Black's translations of Goethe in this context is to find yourself blinking like an owl at a sunnier, hedonistic world. The poet defies the Gods to rival his lusty pleasures, or at a roadside inn curses his inability to consummate the seduction of the maid, or taps out hexameters on his Roman mistress's back. Although there are moments when the meter becomes mechanical, Black's versions of the *Roman Elegies*, particularly, are spirited and entertaining and we sense the Nordic mind unwinding where "the moon gives more light…than mid-day in the North!" and where a "bundle of brushwood" that "falls into cinders and fades" is presage of further sensual pleasures and not a chilling symbol of fascism.

Jamie McKendrick is the Editor of *The Faber Book of 20th-Century Italian Poems*; *Ink Stone* was published in 2003. *Crocodiles & Obelisks* is due to be published in 2007.

A Post-Lapsarian World

DANIELLE CHAPMAN

C.D.Wright, *Like Something Flying Backwards*,
Bloodaxe, £12, ISBN 9781852247621;
Paul Auster, *Collected Poems*, Faber, £16.99, ISBN 9780571234967

Anyone who's lived in, read about, or listened to the music of the American South knows that it's a place of its own peculiar misery, but the way C.D.Wright writes about being down-and-out almost makes it seem like news, as in the poem 'Libretto', which ends:

> A girl sits out-of-doors in her slip.
> She turns fourteen, twenty-eight, fifty-six,
> goes crazy.
>
> The saxophone plays it for somebody else.

Play hell.

This disarmingly frank, ballsy voice isn't coming from a bluegrass singer, but, surprisingly enough, from one of the superstars of American academe. It's not unusual for a Wright poem about, say, "a night or two in the pokey" to also incorporate terms like "ontogeny" and "etiolating" without the slightest hesitation (140). At its best, her marriage of the academy and the Ozarks (she's originally from Arkansas) becomes a strategy through which she uses America's odd-sounding vernacular to expose it as a place of infuriating contradictions and bizarre beauty.

Extremity is Wright's sensibility, and it regularly leads her to a weird brilliance at the very edges of human experience. In order to get through the thicket with her, a reader must tolerate a sprawling ambition (she seems to write books of poetry rather than poems); random snippets of postmodern theory-speak, Spanish, Latin, and whatever other sound bytes she can forage; acts of nearly pornographic navel-gazing; and a slightly exploitative tendency to trawl the trailer park for the most shocking specimens of humanity. However, once we're there, in her "kingdom of cling peaches, fireworks, red ants," (218) we watch her receive, as revelation, scenes that most of us (shamefully, perhaps) would pass by as too quotidian or disturbing for a poem. The greatest satisfaction for a reader is the specificity of her strangeness: saying of a chicken, "They found her a good home / with a peahen for fellowship" (199); titling a poem to a girlfriend 'Cervical Jazz' (188); or summing up the atmosphere in a pool hall with: "The jukebox in the din calls the man a blanketyblankblank."(209) She's able to lift a phrase or an object out of the air and plunk it into a poem, putting a whole place, a whole set of relationships and circumstances – a whole society – into context.

There's no doubt that the animating devil of Wright's poems – and, indeed, her South is a place where the Devil still exists – is in its details. But she's drawn to Big Ideas as much as any other poet. (Think of Shelley's "Spirit of Beauty"; or of William Carlos Williams's dictum, "no ideas but in things," a pretty hefty idea in itself.) Really, a poetry without abstraction is just as impoverished as a poetry without specifics. Yet, the best poems usually find a way to wrestle lofty concepts into real, tangible, touchable things, thereby illuminating our minds and our senses at once. So how do we read a poet who, though he fervently attempts to 'encounter' the world outside his mind, ultimately does not believe that language can render the world – or even that an actual world exists apart from one's abstract perception of it?

For Paul Auster, the compulsion to speak is the completely sincere, yet completely futile, fate of a poet in a post-lapsarian world. As a born writer and thinker, he has no choice but to form and utter perceptions, and yet he harbours no hope that his language can actually capture experience. While attempts to reach out to an unnamed 'other' – often through the simple scenes before him, like "these spasms / of light, in brittle fern, in dark / thickets" (45) or "Grappled flesh / of the fully other" (67) – may result in momentary revelations, they soon exile the speaker back to his place in the cosmic silence of God's absence. And Auster accepts that; as he writes in 'White Spaces': "If I happen to be speaking at this moment, it is only because I hope to find a way of going along, of running parallel to everything else that is going along, and so to begin to find a way of filling the silence without breaking it."

Auster's poems have been noted for their lyricism, and there is a haunting, though anonymous and rather unvarying, melody that runs beneath every poem in this book. At times, he achieves a lovely, limpid clarity, where every perception of beauty resonates, then disappears, into the pool of nothingness into which it is dropped:

> Autumn: a single leaf
> eaten by light: and the green
> gaze of green upon us.
> Where earth does not stop,
> we, too, will become this light,
> even as the light
> dies
> in the shape of a leaf. ('Pulse')

It is strange, though, how an effort toward such clarity, an elimination of self and motive, can come to bear such a heavy mark. Auster's well-known translations of the French surrealists are also included here, and they, too, are ruled by that same intensely disembodied melody. While he has rendered the essence of these poets in unadorned, pure-sounding English, I can't help but miss the friction, the oddities and distinctions, of a translation in which the temperament of the translator challenges and sparks off of that of the poet. Paul Auster's translations, like most of the poems in this book, often seem less like made things than rites of purification, efforts to test language in its ability to render physical reality – and, ultimately, finding language insufficient to the task, a justification to adopt a more philosophical, novelistic approach to life and to writing. After reading this book, perhaps one should not be surprised that Auster published his last book of poetry in 1979.

Danielle Chapman's recent poems appear in *The Atlantic Monthly* and *The New England Review*. A resident of Chicago, she reviews regularly for *The Chicago Tribune* and *Poetry*.

Masculine Tragedians

STEPHEN ROMER

Brendan Kennelly, *When Then Is Now: Three Greek Tragedies*, Bloodaxe, £9.95, ISBN 1852247436; Ted Hughes, *Selected Translations*, ed. Daniel Weissbort, Faber, £20, ISBN 0571221408; Yusef Komunyakaa and Chad Gracia, *Gilgamesh: A Verse Play*, Wesleyan, No price given, ISBN 0819568244

It is not easy to remove to the harsh light and vehement shadow of Greek tragedy, with its immovable objects and irresistible forces. Even the deadly, but principled, oppositions that Nietzsche taught us to see, and which seem so clarifying, are after all distorted by the arbitrary caprices of the gods. In its essence Greek tragedy remains other: especially the more remote, primitive, chthonic processes of Aeschylus and the inconclusive calm-amidst-the-horror that is Sophoclean... We are perhaps closer to psychologist Euripides, who is more Socratic and quicker to moralize and judge in ways resembling ours. Yet he too lays on horrors; without relief or, in the end, satisfying our nice Augustan notions of poetic justice. The task confronting the poet-translator of these cultural monuments continues to be that described by Eliot in his famous essay 'Euripides and Professor Murray' nearly a century ago: "We need an eye which can see the past in its place with its definite difference from the present, and yet so lively that it shall be as present to us as the present." And there's the rub, for it is extremely hard to strike the balance between an ethical respect for the original (slave-owning Ancient Greece is scarcely even imaginable) and the temptations of 'relevance'.

With its striking cover image of an elegant woman executing theatrical 'movements', and unsubtle title, it's clear from the outset that Brendan Kennelly's *When Then Is Now*, pitches its tent in the camp of 'relevance'. This is further impressed upon us by Kennelly's disarming prefaces, which read like personal confessions. They are remarkable pieces in their way, and useful indicators as to where we should look for fresh emphasis. The volume collects versions of three plays: *Antigone* by Sophocles, and *Medea* and *The Trojan Women* by Euripides. All "focus on women whose lives are torn apart by war, family conflict and despotic regimes". Kennelly's version of *Antigone*, he tells us, "came out of my heart and mind, following marriage break-up", and *Medea* was composed while recovering from alcoholism in, trenchantly enough, Dean Swift's hospital, St Patrick's, Dublin. Kennelly's vision of these two plays, and even more emphatically in that unrelieved catalogue of misery *The Trojan Women*, focuses on the suffering and endurance of women, especially women used and abused by men.

This is all admirable; and who would not support passionate writing, such as this claims to be, "in praise of women". Unfortunately, Kennelly battens his "praise" of women onto the dramas of Sophocles and Euripides. The risk is that this feminist skew disfigures and, worse, vulgarizes, the Greek tragedians. His first effort is probably the most successful. Antigone is the passionate girl who represents the justice owed to *oikos*, the clan, the family, the home, and the dignity owed to the dead, as against the wider, civic justice, crucial to the *raison d'état* and the preservation of the *polis* embodied in the person of Creon. Is this Bernadette Devlin on the burning plains of Thebes? The "intimate, tribal revenge" that Heaney wrote of, in a direct evocation of the Troubles? Creon is merely a fool, heavy-handed in his tactics and misogynist with it: Kennelly overstates Sophocles to make the point –

> While I live, no woman
> Will tell me how to think and feel;
> Above all, how to rule. I know how to rule.
> That's why I know I am not a fool.

The lameness of the rhymes, and the generally broken-backed rhythm, might at first appear aptly mimetic of Creon's lame reasoning. But there is altogether too much of this casual half-accidental rhyming, even in the opening exchanges between Antigone and her sister Ismene, to convince:

> I knew it perfectly well.
> That's why I brought you out here,
> Out of that court of sinister stone,
> Where you can hear the word
> All on your own.

I am curious as to how these rhymes – clearly employed to skivvy the verse along, and to give it a semblance of 'structure' – actually sounded on the stage of the Abbey Theatre. Kennelly does better with the choral lyrics; and when Creon, with hubristic relish, sets out the terms of the troublemaker's doom: "I will take her to the loneliest place in the world. / It is a hole among the rocks, / A black pit of emptiness. / But she must live forever / In that dark hole, blacker than any midnight."

It is with Euripides that Kennelly lets rip, so to speak, and puts into the mouths of Medea, already a viciously articulate man-hater, and the Trojan Women, language and formulations quite unwarranted by the Greek. I have nothing against 'Imitation', if in the end it does honour to its original. But where Medea – to paraphrase more literal translations – deplores the lot of woman who must, at great price, find a husband to set himself up as the "ruler of her body", and with whom she has the still greater difficulty of learning to live, Kennelly goes on an extraordinary riff:

> First, all dressed in white, for the most part,
> we are the playthings of men's bodies,
> the sensual toys of tyrants.
> Men, the horny despots of our bodies,
> sucking, fucking, licking, chewing, farting into our skin,
> sitting on our faces, fingering our arses,
> exploring our cunts, widening our thighs,
> drawing the milk that gave the bastards life.

This reads to me like inverted sexism, like male guilt speaking; the pseudo-repentance of the maudlin (reformed) alcoholic. In his Preface, Kennelly reveals, to his credit, the reactions he got to *Medea*. While most admired it, and shared Medea's loathing for the cold-hearted, "yuppified" and "plausible" Jason, "some women thought the play was a diatribe against women, the work of a woman-hater who didn't recognize his own hate". The truth is that the crudest accusations are free additions by Brendan Kennelly himself. These foul-mouthed speeches lessen our sympathy for the wronged heroine; surely not the intention. This is even more egregiously so in *The Trojan Women*, where the translator takes upon himself to put foul language into the mouth of the venerable grieving Hecuba herself, the aged spouse of the dead king Priam. I hate to use the word, but to have Hecuba, who is after all an aged matron who has just been prevented from staggering alive into the flames of Troy, fantasize about being rummaged by

Odysseus, really is 'inappropriate'…

There is a different energy at work in the versions of Aeschylus and Euripides by Ted Hughes, or in the excerpts reproduced in his *Selected Translations*, edited (with illuminating annotation) by Daniel Weissbort. This is an important book, indispensable for students of Hughes, revealing as it does how the activity of translation continually fed his own creativity, not only in the later years with the classical translations (*Tales from Ovid*, notably, and from the Greek) but also in the 'sixties and 'seventies, the early 'heroic' years of *Modern Poetry in Translation* (which he at first co-edited with Weissbort). These were the years of Poetry International, and of the UK's discovery of poets like Hungarians Juhasz and Pilinszky or the Israeli Amichai, all of whom Hughes translated, painstakingly, from interlinear cribs. Concentrating on versions from Greek and Latin, Hughes shares with Kennelly the modernizing instinct to shed mythological allusion and genealogies. Even more than Kennelly, he 'cuts to the chase': often the goriest moments. But where Kennelly gives a political slant – frequently using slack-measured catch-all rhythm and heterogeneous language to do so – intensity and exactness of rhythm, limitation and concentration of language are the very heart of Hughes's enterprise. His radically stripped-down versions are carved out of cadenced breath, and silence:

> my country rots   but it isn't the gods
> it is this   a son and a mother
> knotted and twisted together   a son and a mother
> blood flowing back together in the one sewer
> it isn't the wind fevers from the south of your dried out
>   earth   the drought and its scorching dust
> those things are innocent
> it is your king

A quarter of a century later, tackling the *Oresteia* for the National Theatre, Hughes seems to have lost nothing of his appetite, or his gift for compactness and concentration. His Cassandra is predictably creepier and more blood-boltered than anyone else's:

> She is washing her husband
> In his own blood.
> He reaches from the bath for her hand
> As it jerks him into pitch darkness.

[...]
Now the net – the fish-eye terror:
Death is bundling him up, like a mother
Swaddling a child.
The woman who shared his bed
Is driving the bronze through him.

Hughes explained to Leonard Baskin that he wanted to "release the howl in every line". This is the poet with the volume turned up, and the dinning can bring on migraine. But the wonder is that we are able to take so much, and admire it, before the ache sets in.

Ted Hughes was, to a greater degree than any other poet of his age, versed in Creation Myth, and it was both the strength and the weakness of his poems, especially the later ones, that he was so prepared to deploy the great Myth in his personal poems, where we may find, for example, the Terrible Mother, Inanna or Coatlicue, going quietly mad in Clapham. In fact, his imagination and his sympathies ran to cultures more remote than the Greek, (he calls the people in Seneca "more primitive than aboriginals. They are a spider people, scuttling among hot stones") and he was fascinated by the "raw and strange" transcriptions of Bushmen lore, a scrupulous literalism by an anthropologist which, according to Weissbort, Hughes considered an ideal model for translation. He mentions characters from the *Gilgamesh* cycle, that great epic which pre-dates Homer by at least 1500 years. This is a tale of power, the abuse of power, the discovery of mortality, and the testing of a hero, who tries, and fails, to vanquish death by visiting the underworld, or the other-world, or at least to meet him on his own terms, man-to-man, or: "Toehold to toehold, / eyeball to eyeball, / measure to measure, I believe / you are the one I have been searching for."

This is Gilgamesh to Enkidu, during their memorable war-embrace, the embrace between a half-god half-man and a half-man half-animal, meeting in their shared suffering mysterious substance, man. In place of the usual prose collation from the heterogeneous mass of cuneiform tablets, the poet Yusef Komunyakaa and dramaturge Chad Gracia have re-imagined the ancient Sumerian tale as a verse drama, composed of a series of confrontations brought alive by very fine writing, an impressive lyrical terseness. Pages of "begats" are reduced to a nicely meta-textual moment from the Chorus, "And we sing to you / all the old begats / up the Tigris and Euphrates", and the rhetorical divagations on the properties of the gods, or of the splendid Master of the Cedars, Humbaba, are largely put aside. The gain is in dramatic power (this is, after all, a verse play). Gilgamesh emerges as a man on a painful journey to (at least partial) self-knowledge. His own mortality is a first lesson, as he grieves for his dead blood-brother Enkidu:

> And I sit here –
> till –
> till one day
> turns into three –
> and I cannot stop
> staring at Death
> till a maggot
> drops from Enkidu's
> nose.

Gilgamesh was a historical ruler of Uruk, in present-day Iraq, but here there is – thankfully – no forced attempt at 'relevance'; rather, this translation is a reminder, if we needed one, of how extraordinarily rich and inventive the ancient Mesopotamian civilization was. Gilgamesh is chastened, a wiser and a sadder man at the end of his Epic. The poet of the Myth, and the Greek tragedians also, remind us, with a mixture of despair and awe, that we are strangers to ourselves and to each other.

The poet Stephen Romer is the Editor of *Twentieth Century French Poems* (Faber, 2002).

Our Principal Anthropologist

MICHAEL HULSE

David Harsent, *Selected Poems 1969-2005*, Faber, £11.99, ISBN 9780571234011

Only quite recently, with a rack of prizes and shortlistings including the PBS Choice for *A Bird's Idea of Flight* (1998) and, two books later, the T.S. Eliot and Whitbread shortlists and Forward Prize for Best Collection for *Legion* (2005), has David Harsent become properly visible, and been praised in a manner proportionate to his achievement.

Partly, as this selection confirms, this is because it wasn't till the Eighties that Harsent found his mature voice, in the extraordinary sequence *Mister Punch* (1984); partly it's because he doesn't often do the epiphany poem or the life's-like-that poem or the Poems in the Underground poem; partly it's because he's always been a darker sort of horse (whether by personal preference or promoters' oversight I can't say) than those that fuel public notice, from *Poetry Please* to the school curricula.

That said, the steady emergence of David Harsent as one of the strongest voices in contemporary English poetry still needs accounting for in some other way. It's clear that, like Hugo Williams a few years before him, Harsent didn't get off to a *Hawk in the Rain* kind of start. His first couple of books, like Williams's, gave little indication of the mastery-with-modesty that was to come. "The women are dark and seem / very beautiful; the men / look nervous, overdressed. / It's always summer, where they stand, / arms linked, facing the sun, / their blurred smiles meant for no one," runs the entirety of 'Old Photographs' (in *After Dark*, 1973). The knowing generalisation, the studied understatement of the diction and syntax, the modulation to a near-bathetic plangency in the last line, are very much of the period.

But then, a decade later, the tone has been transformed into this:

> Is Punch a killer? Nights alone in the house
> leave him shaken and sick.
> Prowlers pad the blistered alleyways;
> lean and angry, their nerves strung tight,
> they own the streets and carve out what they want.
> He seems to hear
> her voice, a murmur, almost out of earshot
> in one of the rooms where her things still lie about.

The line is sharper, the syntax broader, the subject matter better focussed and textured. Tired of laconic restraint, Harsent in *Mister Punch* has relaxed and started to follow the instincts that govern his later work: letting the line determine its own length and pliability, and allowing an uncensored voice to the darkness within.

The darkness is the great subject; human darkness, individual, collective. From the male "homunculus" fired by "the thug within the skin", whose heart is "inarticulate and murderous and mad", Harsent moved via the First World War (*News from the Front*, 1993) to the chamber of horrors and quests-for-perfection that make up *A Bird's Idea of Flight*. Poem by poem, that collection raises the hairs on the neck. The subjects are mainly grim (garotting, the guessed-at victim stowed in a vintner's cellar, a brain plopped into a brass bowl in an early anatomy lesson); they are no less grim for being intimately involved with the advance of civilisation, its pleasure and knowledge as much as its discontents.

Always in the grimness, Harsent's major-key rhythms work enigmatic and paradoxical miracles. An outstanding poem in the fiercely-titled *Legion* recalls the "man who made toffee" and the "man who made small / animals […] from scraps of steel" and the "man who made paintings" before concluding,

> […] I thought that if I could find him,
> or one of the other two, or any in that street, I might know
> what became of my house and those in it; and what to do;
> and where to go.

The implied history of conflict, loss, and disorientation, could have settings in many heartbreaking places in recent years. Even so, hope lurks defiant. The opening down-beat of that last line modulates to an almost up-beat (and rhyming) close: as long as the speaker is wondering where to go, s/he is wondering about a future.

The fact is, David Harsent has become a poet of immense power, nuance and resource, enriching his textures with 'high' culture and with folk and ballad features, pursuing uncompromising insights and rigorous narratives, laying down rhythms as deft as any in Robert Gray or Paul Muldoon. How then to account for the tardiness of his wider recognition? The thought raises questions of dominance in the poetic landscape. Larkin had to die before Duffy and Armitage were empowered to emerge. And only with Ted Hughes gone could our principal anthropologist come into his own: Harsent is our master of the human red in tooth and claw.

Michael Hulse's latest translation is *Berlin* (Taschen). He is a judge of the Günter Grass Foundation's Albatross Prize.

The Clear Note

RUTH FAINLIGHT

Galway Kinnell, *Strong Is Your Hold*, Bloodaxe, £8.95, ISBN 9781852247683;
W.S. Merwin, *Selected Poems*, Bloodaxe, £9.95, ISBN 9781852247690

Anew collection, and a selection from a lifetime's work: new books from two major American poets, both celebrating their eightieth birthdays this year. The parallels and contrasts are fascinating. Both are distinguished translators and recipients of many awards and prizes. Both are environmentalists intimately involved with the natural world – Galway Kinnell from his New England farmhouse, W.S. Merwin from his palm-garden on the Pacific island of Maui. Each book includes a poem dealing with the tragedy of 9/11. Kinnell's 'When the Towers Fell', is a plangent requiem for the victims, after witnessing the collapse of the Twin Towers from his apartment opposite. In an interview in 2001 he stated: "Knowing that what we call evil in others also exists in ourselves at least makes it possible to write something that has some authenticity." Merwin's 'To the Words' is a more oblique response in which he says, as was said about the Holocaust, that such an event is beyond words – yet his poem ends with the two words: "say it".

Kinnell's vocabulary is rich with specific dialect words, obsolete according to the *Complete Oxford*, but very alive as he uses them. *Fulge, prog, glidder, cramble, hirple, clart* are a few examples. Listening to him pronounce them with such obvious pleasure (a CD of him reading is included in the book), deepened my own. Their dense earthy tone is absolutely appropriate for poems which, whatever their starting inspiration, whether the human, animal or vegetable world or the entire universe, are rooted in a profound yet almost jaunty acceptance of the cycles of generation and decomposition, life and death.

In the same spirit, his young daughter, garter snakes slung across her shoulder, shows him where, inside one's mouth, the legs of a frog are being slowly drawn down and:

> Perhaps thinking I might be considering rescue,
> Maud said, "Don't. Frog is already elsewhere."

A superb long poem, 'Pulling a Nail', exemplifies his work at its best. It is a detailed description of his effort to extract a nail from the piece of wood into which it was hammered by his father in the year of Kinnell's birth. At the same time it is an elegy for his father and a celebration of the material world and of the dignity of labour reminiscent of Philip Levine's poetry. There are other moving elegies: memorial poems for poet-friends Jane Kenyon and James Wright, vivid poems about his children, and many love poems, affectionate, sensual and thoughtful as well as very sexy. They are also very witty – like this one, with the unambiguous title 'Sex':

> On my hands are the odors
> of the knockout ether
> either of above the sky
> where the bluebirds get blued
> on their upper surfaces
> or of down under the earth
> where the immaculate nightcrawlers
> take in tubes of red earth
> and polish their insides.

A *Selected* drawing on fifty-five years of work is quite another matter. Few of Merwin's collections go unrepresented in this volume, and although it might have been difficult to extract meaningfully from it, I am sorry that nothing has been included from one of my favourite books of his, the verse-novel *The Folding Cliffs* (1998), a narrative of nineteenth century Hawaii. I add my fervent praise to that of Ted Hughes: "*The Folding Cliffs* is a masterpiece…" Another of my favourites is *The Vixen* (1996), (in which the creature herself is characterised as "sibyl of the extinguished"), set in the austere stern landscape of SW France, where the poet had a house for some years. Memories of WW2 are still potent – in 'The Red' he stumbles upon a stone memorial deep in the oak woods at the site of the shooting of a group of old people and children and the burning of their buildings and animals by retreating German soldiers. There are poems which become meditations on time and memory, such as 'The Speed of Light'; and Virgilian elegies for the lost lives of the French villagers among whom he lived, like 'Fox Sleep' and 'Oak Time':

> no animals are led out any longer from the barns
>> after the milking to spend the night pastured here
> they are all gone from the village Edouard is gone

> who walked out before them to the end of his days
> keeping an eye on the walnuts still green along the road
> when the owl watched from these oaks and in the night
> I would hear the fox that barked here bark and be gone

Merwin's sense of connection with the community of poets, living and dead, is obvious through every collection – from the last two stanzas of his poem 'Berryman' in *Opening the Hand* (1983), (with its message for all writers!):

> I had hardly begun to read
> I asked how can you ever be sure
> that what you write is really
> any good at all and he said you can't
> you can't you can never be sure
> you die without knowing
> whether anything you wrote was any good
> if you have to be sure don't write

– to *The River Sound* (1999), with its 'Lament for the Makers', an *in memoriam* for the poets who have been most important to him, fifty-two brisk quatrains building to a statement equally relevant as the quotation above:

> and the clear note they were hearing
> never promised anything
> but the true sound of brevity
> that will go on after me

The influence of the Spanish poets he was translating then – and has continued to do – is already evident in the earlier books, as in 'The Last One' from *The Lice* (1967), with its evocation of Vallejo, and the tiny Machedo-like three-lined 'Separations' from *The Moving Target* (1963): "Your absence has gone through me / Like thread through a needle. / Everything I do is stitched with its color."

With *The Rain in the Trees* (1988), a growing awareness of approaching death, not merely his own, but that of every form of life on the planet, permeates his work and becomes more and more the subject, expressed here in 'Witness', 'Place', 'Chord' and 'Losing a Language'. And, with *Travels*

(1993), I hear an alteration to structure and syntax which opens the language into a tranced chant which sometimes I had to chant myself before I could really understand. Yet I was intrigued to note that he is still using the traditional forms as masterfully as in his earlier books: two poems in *The Pupil* (2001) and *Present Company* (2005), 'Overtone' and 'To the Dust of the Road', are strict sonnets. Merwin continues to surpass himself as his newest work becomes more simple and resolved, rinsed clear of extraneous material, like poems which might have been written by that exile invoked in 'To a Friend Travelling':

> this is like one of those letters
> written on a mountain
> in China more than
> a thousand years ago
> by someone staring
> at the miles of white clouds
> after a friend's departure
> there were so many of those
> unsigned and never sent
> as far as we know

Ruth Fainlight's latest collection is *Moon Wheels* (Bloodaxe, 2006).

A Total And A Shadow Art

DAVID MORLEY

Medbh McGuckian, *The Currach Requires No Harbour*, The Gallery Press,
£11.95, ISBN 1852354127;
Peter McDonald, *The House of Clay*, Carcanet, £8.95, ISBN 185754871X

Medbh McGuckian has always been a convincingly total artist: a musician and painter who happens to use language as her medium. Some critics stare at her poems as if they were Fermat equations, blinded by their grammatical science. Academics slant her work through prisms of theory, or interpret them as mere extensions of her source reading – whereas what she does time and again is subvert her chosen sources into a kind of pure poetry. Writers are our greatest readers, and it is not unusual to find gleaming fragments of other authors scattered in their works like weapons gripped then dropped in the battle to write.

The wonderful 'Anne Glyd, her Book, 1656' is an example of such a total subversion of material. It is gleaned from Patricia Crawford and Laura Gowring's *Women's Worlds in Seventeenth Century England* (Routledge, 2000), and takes as its cue the often precise and luminous prose of women's commonplace and mothers' advice books. The poem reclaims the voice of women whose role in the community of the time was a great deal more important than history allowed:

> Make thin bowls of lead fit to cover the breast or wen,
> and when you do lay it to the breast, warm it a little,
> and so whelm it and make it fast
>
> that it remove not, and let it lie
> as you feel occasion. An honest woman
> revealed this who had proved it to be true.
>
> And *she* learned it of a poor woman
> that required alms at the door.

Commonplace or advice books sometimes seem a shadow-world, counter-parting the masculine times in which they were composed; but they were vital documents. They are domestic but they represent a poetry of survival. This poem, and several others like it in the book, makes more public a type of women's literature to which scholarship has only recently begun to attend. However, these are poems first: they are not 'found' literature. The language is chosen with tact, added to and lineated with great prosodic skill – and McGuckian is just as skilled in making herself invisible in her work. She also gracefully acknowledges her inspirational sources.

As I said, McGuckian is a total artist; she has something of Emily Dickinson's totality of approach, as well as Dickinson's domestic surrealism. A critic's search for narrative, for meanings, for interpretation, can be a narrow – a narrowing – way of advancing through a book like this. *The Currach Requires No Harbours* is a concentration, rather than a collection, of poems. The work seeks a total attention from the reader. What we as readers could be doing is walking through her works as though they were galleries of abstract textual paintings – and listening to her poems as if they were short movements of a symphony. This book is McGuckian's *Symphony No.11*, the very kind of text that sings out for a CD recording (her clear-eyed publisher Gallery Press should consider this proposition).

McGuckian's poems refract her reading and perception of a shadow-world of dead women writers. You can glimpse the shadows of writers in Peter McDonald's *The House of Clay* but McDonald desires and declares their presence (his Notes underscore the point). 'War Diary' opens with a line from Edward Thomas's journal but takes a Frost-y, bleak swerve:

> […] clear glass is a mirror
> as the night goes up into action
> on wet roads, never to return:
> the country roads long since taken,
> known mile by mile, yard by yard,
> and still abandoned. What did I see there?
> Who, maybe? Some such question.

A sequence, 'The Bees', shadows Virgil's *Georgics*; but the sensuously elegant syntax of the four associated pieces is all Peter McDonald. Within these Virgilian poems – as with others – the poet hazards a single sentence to carry a whole piece; a daring gesture that requires his punctuation to perform with as much energy and precision as any of his words. The result is that the poems seem to grow or flow from their natural subject; long flying language dances through colons, dashes and semi-colons, veering the poem sideways then forwards. It gives the poems great nerve, and McDonald never loses control of the lines as they lean onward on their sound-wings. His similarly fleer 'San Domenico' is a forty-eight-line single sentence which shifts from space to shadowy space, small memory movements and magnetic observation opening and closing "old books of lives, / smoothing their pages, to fill the first leaves / with leaves of bay". It makes for a stunning opening to the book.

I have admired McDonald's poems since his appearance in the *New Chatto Poets* anthology of 1986. That must seem a lifetime ago to a poet who has made considerable artistic progress since – both in his poems and in his criticism. For McDonald, an act of criticism is also an act of creativity; they are the hemispheres of a single world, and criticism illuminates most sharply when practical experience of writing is at the bottom of it. The critic's presence is a necessary balance for the poet's absence:

I might have been a ghost,
a shadow, and not the guest
they had been expecting. ('Late Morning')

As a critic, McDonald has been an unswerving advocate of so-called difficult poets. As a poet he is as uncompromising and perhaps as focussed and as total an artist as Medbh McGuckian. This new book is exceptional: beguiling in its language and structure, it is also very moving in parts, especially the Belfast childhood poems. As with McGuckian's, the whole book is closely and cunningly composed for the mind's ear, as well as the eye.

David Morley's new collection of poetry is *The Invisible Kings*, a PBS Recommendation.

Shall I Stay Or Shall I Go?

CHARLOTTE NEWMAN

Tracy Ryan, *Hothouse*, Arc, £8.99, ISBN 9781904614135;
Gillian Allnutt, *How the Bicycle Shone: New & Selected Poems*,
Bloodaxe, £12, ISBN 9781852247591;
Kapka Kassabova, *Geography for the Lost*, Bloodaxe, £7.95, ISBN 9781852247652

If freedom may be defined by the ability to move freely – be it international travel or taking a first step – to these three poets both freedom and movement are inextricably bound up with femininity. Tracy Ryan's *Hothouse* explores what-it-means-to-be-female by drawing on the differences between the human world and the plant world. It is in considering what for Ryan is the fundamental difference, before consciousness necessarily enters the picture, between plants and humans – the involuntary stasis of plants set against the physical ability for humans to move – that this collection achieves a defining sense of difficulty.

This tension manifests itself in every detail down to the use of tense and choice of where to place verbs on the page. The touchstone is the past participle, with its sense of distance and cool detachment; there is contingency in the playing-off of moods and tenses: terms of fixity following words of uncertainty, transparency opacity. Language is mimetic, as in 'On-line':

> and should I want
>
> to evade, I could pretend
> her words never arrived
>
> left to hang
> like that message
>
> from a friend who died
> hours later
>
> that I could not delete.

The line-ending has two functions: as a note of finality curtailed by the "-ed", or as an edge to "hang" uncertainties upon. With these equivocations comes a meditation on communication and its limits, expressed through the invocation of plants as models of taciturnity. As animals are introduced, in poems like 'The Peacocks', diametrical opposition is complicated, opening up a compendium of tensions between different species of organic life. The short line is a unit that Ryan favours, and she must make it work harder in order to justify the disruption to the poems' fluidity. In the fourth section of 'The Peacocks', abrupt endings and shifting lineation successfully convey ambivalence within a flower's necessary inertia:

> Finely perverse
> > in your resistance
> to placement,
> > thing or being
>
> sky-formed surely yet
> > earth-indued
> weighed down with
> > fantastic garland

The language of restraint and coercion is necessarily sexual, and it is at this point that ideas of gender boundaries, and of relative freedoms, become important. Ryan's *Hothouse* predominantly houses flowers; with their wealth of individual symbolisms. Mad Ophelia with her apothecary – full of herbal garlands – and along with that her sexual repression – appears in 'Hyacinths'. Being bound to the earth as a flower is Ryan's updating of this image: while Ophelia's flowers are uprooted, Ryan's hyacinths are bound "to black earth and / incredulity"; while Ophelia rushes past to escape a mysterious "attacker", the flowers can only remain static and stoic where they grow. For Ryan, the essential paradox of plants, it seems, is that while they cannot move as we do, they do grow, upwards, phototropically.

Movement within space is something Gillian Allnutt explores further in *How the Bicycle Shone*, a *New and Selected Poems* spanning twenty-six years. She moves within both geographical and typographical space and explores both simultaneously. Her poetry is well-travelled, settling especially in the north of England and biblical backdrops; the breadth of her literary and mythical allusions is also a kind of expression of freedom: the poet is at liberty to move among her own inspirations. Allnutt draws on sources as diverse as mediaeval lyric poetry and nursery rhymes, resulting in an idiosyncratic ability to interpolate other texts, as well as allowing her to indulge in both parody and pastiche. This works on the micro-level of the phrase, in Hopkins-like archaisms: "For this rose-engravéd anchor", or more subtly in individual lines, or complete poems. There are moments where one can detect strong notes of late Wallace Stevens: "I'll forget / how I fought imagination. Was it my own / indisputable angel?"

This can be followed through to the Stevensian – and also Lowellian – titles of individual collections included here, particularly *Nantucket and the Angel*. But despite the Lowell-like premise, Allnutt eschews any 'confessional' tone in favour of myth-making, or straightforward, non-narcissistic storytelling. The real debt to both Lowell and Stevens lies in her use of religiosity as a mainstay as well as a trope to twist into a new kind of metaphysical discourse: "Life with you, Gabriel she says is unnecessarily complicated. / Like a grace note." ('Table') Here, in a poem that brings together Christ, Beethoven and Emily Dickinson to a kind of transhistorical Last Supper, Allnutt demonstrates both how one can beat Steven's "necessary angel of earth", and indirectly pervert his poetic sentiment.

There is an angel in almost every poem, and Gabriel is the guardian; his name after all, we are reminded, is nothing more than "the word for morning". But later in the book, these celestial-earthly movements representing a traditional kind of lyricism give way to a sparse, quasiimagist style that follows a more sound-propelled formula. Terse and laconic, the poems share something of Tracy Ryan's broken-edged cadences; but their sense is ritualistic, witchy even, with the frequent use of "bone" imagery as if the word were some poetic rune. It is a word that finds its way into the entire span of this book, whether or not its use feels apt in every situation. The late poems are pictorial; painterliness is another career-spanning trait, which intensifies in the last collection, *Wolf Light*. These poems are voiced landscapes, occasionally bleak and lonely, as in 'the road to alston' – Allnutt develops an apparent suspicion of capitalisation here – "where neither car nor horse-drawn vehicle". The lack of a concluding verb leaves us hanging on a sense of dissatisfaction that, like the landscape, is resistant to kinesis. There is a tension, in Gillian Allnutt's poetry, between movement on a small scale and displacement on a geographical scale.

Kapka Kassabova, on the other hand, represents the embodiment of the physically wandering woman; the very title of her book suggests the tensions and contradictions inherent in someone who has moved about so freely in terms of travel, but who has struggled to find any kind of identity; although Kassabova does not set herself on a particularly gender-conscious tone. The essential question asked by the collection is whether geographical and emotional exile are analogous, or indeed, are they cause-and-effect? Like both Ryan and Allnutt, these senses of displacement and exile – whether they be due to movement or inertia – are transfigured into language itself, and how, especially in a multilingual context, it may be alienating rather than communicative: "I often think of Mister Hu / who didn't know the word for pun." There is again, an exploration of the limits of communication, although for Kassabova these limits are primarily linguistic, and may be overcome by "gestures". The final part of the collection is a short prose piece describing the multicultural difficulties of her upbringing which details, with the kind of clarity that characterises the whole book, her experience of the plight of tourist and immigrant.

The wandering woman is poetic protagonist of all three of these collections. For Gillian Allnutt, Mary Magdalene recurs as a favourite character; here Allnutt's terseness becomes thoroughly appropriate, exhibiting disdain for the ambivalence surrounding this figure by the short, sharp linguistic contradictions:

> with her pound of ointment

very costly –

Common, prostitute.

A well-known peripatetic and outcast whose loyalty is firmly rooted in one place, the Magdalene embodies the contradictions immanent in womanhood as they are explored in the work of these three poets. It is apt in reading these poetries to consider that our understanding of such literary or historical figures comes to us through the written word, which is, paradoxically, both static and mutable: physically fixed in ink, but subject to renewed interpretation.

Charlotte Newman recently graduated from Selwyn College, Cambridge.

Has *Vers Libre* Won?

DANIEL WEISSBORT

Remco Campert, *I Dreamed In The Cities At Night*, trans. Donald Gardner, introd. by Paul Vincent, Arc Visible Poets, £9.99, ISBN 9781604614364; Mursuo Takahashi, *We of Zipangu*, trans. James Kirkup and Tamaki Makoto, introd. by Glyn Purslove, Arc Visible Poets, £9.99, ISBN 9781904614043; ed. Brane Mozetic, *Six Slovenian Poets*, Arc, £10.99, ISBN 9781904614173; ed. David Morley and Leonard-Daniel Aldead, *No Longer Poetry: New Romanian Poetry*, The Heaventree Press, ISBN 9780954881153

Much of the pleasure of editing *Modern Poetry in Translation* was in finding poets, either in anthologies, where they might be represented by only a handful of poems, or in literal cribs. What drew me was always a certain clarity. The poetry of Eastern Europe seemed to translate well, because it was so lucid, if not unambiguous. No subject was taboo or non-poetic and indeed this was often treated as primary material. Poetry, we learnt, could survive even in severely inimical circumstances. There was also another Europe; now embraced, so to speak, by the Soviet Eurasian landmass. We felt we were imaginatively reconstructing a lost culture.

Arc's new anthology of six Slovenian poets reminds me that in 1970 *MPT*, still edited by Ted Hughes and myself, published an issue dedicated to

Slovenia. At the time, Slovenia had just become an 'independent' republic within Tito's Yugoslavia. Our aim was to draw attention to a distinct literature and language that only *seemed* to have vanished. We 'discovered' fourteen poets, including Edvard Kocbek, a major European figure. The editorial contained basic information: "Slovenia [...] has always, in fact, regarded itself as belonging to Western European culture: the post-war period of Stalinist domination, [...] represents very much of a cultural aberration [...]". Confidence in the cultural distinctiveness of West Europe might be harder to replicate today in the days of a money-dominated European Union, but it was our belief that literally dozens of significant voices had been silenced. Now I am sceptical.

None of the names from that edition of *MPT* appears in this anthology edited by Brane Mozetic, a poet, writer, translator as well as editor. Interestingly, Mozetic graduated in Comparative Literature from the University of Ljubljana. All the poets in the anthology have an academic background, very different to what we found back in the Sixties. It seems that the Cold War has been succeeded by a shift of the cultural centre to the universities. When I was teaching at the University of Iowa, the Chair of Comparative Literature informed me that he had once been in Creative Writing but had transferred to Comparative Literature, with its focus on French critical theory, where, he insisted, all the truly creative work was being done.

I feel, as may already be evident, somewhat remote from the poets of the new era. The poetry of the first post-war East European generation that captured my interest was political and employed a virtually obligatory Aesopian language. Today's poetry is less public, much of it concerned with sex and relationships between private individuals. Everything, too, is in *vers libre* and I ask myself whether this is because free verse has won, so to speak; or because the loss suffered in the translation process is less catastrophic when formal considerations are not so insistent? A kind of internationalism is apparent; a sort of translational activity, if you like, at grass roots level. The Romanian anthology is titled *No Longer Poetry*; which reminds me of the rejection of "poetry" in the post-War European period. Perhaps the process has continued further than one might perhaps have wished, so that it is almost a sine qua non that poetry is "no longer poetry", whatever it may be. Having got that off my chest, I should like to add a positive word about what evidently is happening in this book: a genuine opening up after such a long, politically-imposed stifling of feeling, of human concern. If it is sometimes familiar to us, that is no doubt our good fortune.

But two other books, neither relating to Eastern Europe, are on my table! For many years, James Kirkup has been our premier translator of Japanese poetry, and I was glad to see his selection of poems by the Japanese poet Matsuo Takahashi, in the excellent *Arc Visible Poets* series edited by Jean Boase-Beier, which seeks to showcase rather than camouflage the strange: "[T]he translator of the poets in this series aim not to hide but to reveal the original, to make it visible and in so doing, to render visible the translator's task too." Kirkup might concur. In 'Translating Penna and Cernuda' (*Translating Poetry: The Double Labyrinth*, ed. Weissbort, 1989) he wrote: "I keep as close as possible [...] I dislike those modern poets who seek to impose their own (often interior) individual style and vocabulary on some helpless foreign poet. I try to let the foreign poet speak out in his own way, with his own voice, at the risk of my English occasionally sounding a little strange. [...] Translation into English is a problem of English, not of the foreign language." It is customary for reviewers to find connections between disparate works, but Takahashi has little in common with the younger poets of Eastern Europe. The inclusion of this book in the Arc series is a mark of the editors' eclecticism. It may fairly be said, by now, that this series takes up where Penguin abruptly left off in its *Modern European Poets* series.

Finally, a word about the selection of recent poems by Remco Campert, also in the *Arc Visible Poets* series. Sensibly, this usually bilingual series is not bilingual with Takahashi but, of course, remains so with Campert: Dutch being very close to English, so that it is possible to follow Campert in both languages. He is a poet of clarity and irony, even at times despairingly aphoristic ("At last poetry is free / no one reads it any more") But he also writes at greater length, without surrendering any of his lucidity. His poetry focuses, in a matter-of-fact manner on the everyday. This is a book full of *désabusé* wisdom; expertly conveyed by the translator, Donald Gardner.

Daniel Weissbort's recent publications include *Ted Hughes, Selected Translations* reviewed on pp. 88-93.

ENDPAPERS

❧

As the number of survivors who can talk about Nazi genocide dwindles, the importance of the writing they left us increases. I believe that translating my great-aunt's work is an essential act of witness.

—*Sybil Ruth*

EDITORIAL

FIONA SAMPSON

One reason so much poetry gets written in hospitals and prisons must be that it opens a series of escape hatches. What these give onto probably varies: the heightened diction of inner life; idealised values; a time and place where things are happening differently... *Where do you want to go today?* But the short, sharp shock of a poem offers every reader momentary escape: from another bad day at the office, over-work, the domestic round. No wonder *Poems on the Underground* proved so popular. And small wonder either, then, that British poetry has a distinguished history of dreaming of 'Elsewhere': one that includes Keats "looking into" Chapman's *Homer* and Coleridge experimenting with Kubla Khan; Milton's *Paradise Lost* no less than Gwyneth Lewis's space-travel (in *Zero Gravity*); not to mention the cathartic presence of Mediterranean culture, from *The King James Bible* to Shakespeare.

We can also, of course, read poetry which originates beyond these islands. You'd think that, in a globalised world, this would be uncontentious. Surely it's obvious how our sixty-odd million merely play a part in a world population of six point six billion? Plainly, ours can't be the only culture producing poetry today. But beware: here be dragons. There are obstacles to such cheerful readerly internationalism: 'translation wars' over what a translated poem, that necessary hybrid, represents; academics who claim that only reading in the original is permissible (thus closing off most world literature: show me the scholar who's fluent in Russian, Aramaic, Arabic, German, Greek *and* Mandarin); Poetry Police busy maintaining that writing which doesn't conform to contemporary British fashion fails; and, not least, the consensus that translated poetry is different from poetry *proper*. It can require a certain steadiness to persevere.

Yet, as this issue of *Poetry Review* demonstrates, there's enormous vitality in international writing. Indeed, it's a fair bet that you've got this far without worrying too much that many of the *Poems*, the lion's share of *Centrefold* and nearly all the *Reviews* are international in origin: while our usual *Letter from* abroad has been replaced by two *Postcards from* the UK. International writing is the context of excellence in which the best British poetry sits; *PR* is committed to this vision. This issue, though, consciously celebrates the recent flowering of a translation culture, among our leading poets, analogous to that found elsewhere in the literary world. Without the curiosity, excitement, engagement – and sheer thickening-up of serious literary practice – such work entails, our local poetry will inevitably turn in ever-decreasing circles. *Vive la différence!*

POSTCARD FROM HULL

DAVID WHEATLEY

The presiding spirit of British Poetry is called Eikon Basilike and he lives in a disused mill in Hull. Let me explain. The city's full name, Kingston-upon-Hull, was bestowed on it by Charles I. When he turned up again in 1642 hoping to get his hands on the city's arsenal he was refused entry by a group of Parliamentarians, who met in the "plotting parlour" of a pub called The Old White Harte, in a decision seen as triggering the Civil War that followed. This nexus of Catholic and Protestant, royalist and republican, forms a molten core of historical Englishness in my mind, as expressed in Peter Didsbury's marvellous poem 'Eikon Basilike', in which the ghost of the dead king is last seen taking refuge in a power station. By this, I have arbitrarily decided, Didsbury means the hulking mass of the British Extracting Co. building on the banks of the river Hull. Looking up at it with my camera, I scan hopefully for the peregrine falcons I've heard are nesting on its summit, but they're a no-show today. The Rix Owl lies at anchor below a nearby swing bridge, astride which a pagoda-like structure sits improbably in the air.

My Hull poetry associates Cliff Forshaw, David Kennedy and Christopher Reid and I are engaged on a commission called *Architexts*, in which we write about Hull buildings and match them to the photographs we've been taking on our various peregrinations around the Old Town and the Hull river corridor. I am much taken with England's smallest window, in a pub called The George in the evocatively named Land of Green Ginger. Until quite recently the George who fluttered on the pub sign was no beefy Hanoverian but, of all people, George Eliot. This visit finds monarchical order restored, but I am richly compensated by the intestinal maze of passageways on every side, one of them embossed with an enormous slithering eel, doing his bit for the city's pavement fish A-Z.

Further down the river corridor are a C17th charterhouse once run by Andrew Marvell's father, and a pub and brewery, The Whalebone, where weary psycho-geographers can light a wood fire and sup their pints off poetry beer-mats. One of the in-house beers is named Truelove, after the whaling ship that brought a pair of Inuit children, Memiadluk and Uckaluk, back from the Davis Straits in 1847. They were exhibited in Hull and York before being returned home the following year, only for the girl, Uckaluk, to die of measles on the way. A double bust of their heads near the river's flood barrier bears painful witness to the immigrants' stories that are such a part of the tidal flux and reflux of Hull's identity too.

Close by is a sculpture marking Hull's links with Iceland, which I had suspected (rightly, to judge by my conversations with old trawler-men) were exclusively hostile. When the Icelandic President turned up for the sculpture's unveiling in one of the gunboats that had been used to ram Hull trawlers in the Cod War, the occasion was marked by yet more commissioned poetry, confirming the Scandinavian links visible in Hull streets named after Swedish cities and even the composer Sibelius. There was a third party to the conflict, of course; but the only fishy representatives present had come in the form of a finger buffet.

The list of Hull poets is a long one, from Andrew Marvell to Stevie Smith, Larkin, Dunn, Didsbury and O'Brien, to the more recent generation of blow-ins. Yet unlike the other city I know best, Dublin, Hull retains a peculiar innocence in the face of its literary heritage. No city could be freer of a poetic anxiety of influence. Writing disapprovingly of Rome, the young James Joyce compared its inhabitants' exploitation of its glorious past to exhibiting the embalmed corpse of one's grandmother for a living. Larkin may have a plaque in the branch of Marks & Spencer whose ladies' knickers department he immortalised, but it will be a long time before Hull's literary heritage translates into the kind of tourist tat that Dublin's dead titans have become in their birthplace. To those who have never visited, Hull may seem like the end of the line, a vague remnant of impoverished Northern-ness teetering on the edge of the M62. This suits me just fine. If Hull is the secret poetry capital of England, it would rather not let on that it knows. But the figure flitting back from the pub over the swing bridge towards his disused mill – he knows.

Architexts (Hull City Council, 2007). http://www.flickr.com/photos/larkincentre

☙

POSTCARD FROM LEWIS

ANDREW MITCHELL

"Bayble is a strange name," you said. "You mean the place where both Iain Crichton Smith and Derick Thomson grew up on the Island of Lewis?" I replied. "It's Bayble in English and Pabail in Gaelic. Paba means priest. It's derived from Old Norse, 'place of the priest.'" Then you said, "This is completely lost in English!" I laughed, saying it reminded me of Iain's "The Highlander who loses his language / Loses his world."

It's not about substituting one word for another, but about layers of meaning, accretions over many generations linking place, myth and legend. If you were to summarize Gaelic culture in one word, it would be *ceilidh*. Not the dances you go to in the city, but its Gaelic meaning, the coming together of a whole community; traditionally in a thatched black house, with a central fire round which everyone gathered, to sing, dance, play music, tell stories and recite poetry. This oral tradition has always been under threat. Land tenure was traditionally precarious; and when the Established Church backed the landowners over evictions the Islanders converted en masse to the Free Church. This didn't stop the evictions, nor the Clearances, but added other issues: over-zealous ministers fired with Calvinistic fervour demanded an end to singing, dancing and all music. As Thomson says, "and he swept the fire from the centre of the floor / and set a searing bonfire in our breasts".

The advent of wage-earning heralded the Celtic Diaspora; there weren't enough paid jobs. Education, conducted in English, assisted this dispersal, as it did in Wales and Ireland: children spoke Gaelic in the playground and English in class. The decline recorded in the 1961 Census prompted Derick to remember the funeral of his grandfather, a joiner who also made coffins, thirty years before:

I did not recognise the English braid,
the Lowland varnish being applied to the wood,
I did not read the words on the brass,
I did not understand that my race was dying.

Declining crofting communities remain the bedrock of spoken Gaelic and, despite many laudable initiatives, especially in education, Gaelic-speakers in the 2001 Census fell below 60,000 (to 58,000) for the first time. In 1891 there were 210,000.

Both Iain Crichton Smith and – six years older – Derick Thomson, each writing principally in their second language, were haunted by and gave expression to the cultural concerns of their childhood home; yet both effectively left the Island when they went to university. Iain forever balanced what he called the English and Gaelic wheels of the bicycle he rode; Derick fixed upon the Gaelic culture he was determined to defend.

Derick Thomson, Iain Crichton Smith & Andrew Mitchell, *Taking You Home: poems and conversations* (Argyll Publishing).

ℬ

Translating Theresienstadt

SIBYL RUTH

I have begun translating poetry written by my great-aunt Rose Scooler. The poems date from 1944–5, when she lived in Theresienstadt, the concentration camp, north of Prague, also known as Terezin.

I've spent a long time preparing to be a translator. Since childhood I've been trying to make sense of my elders' words, to build them into a coherent narrative. Sometimes, I was offered stories that seemed almost complete – like my mother's tales of idyllic summers in the home of her mother's sister, Tante Rose, who had a big house in Saxony. I'd imagine Tante Rose as a kind of queen because my mother had to greet her with a curtsey.

My mother didn't teach me to speak her native tongue. Maybe she preferred to keep this for private conversations with her own mother. And in 1960's suburban Cheshire, she might have worried about German-speaking children not fitting in. But at night my grandmother always said *Gute Nacht* to me. In the morning she'd ask, *Hast du gut geschlafen?*

In my teens and twenties, I was filling in gaps. For my Jewish forebears Hitler's growing power changed everything. Tante Rose had to sell the family business. Her son Walter was registered as a "half-Jew", so living with him afforded protection. But when he was called up into a forced labour battalion, my great-aunt was sent to Theresienstadt.

The camp presented itself to the outside world as a model settlement. To this end, a charade of cultural life was permitted. Tante Rose, then in her early sixties, worked in a "home" for the elderly, and later in a workshop splitting mica. It was here she composed and memorised poems, as a way of enduring monotony and long shifts. The labour saved her life. Mica was used in the making of planes; those who prepared it were spared transportation to death camps. So my great-aunt lived to celebrate her hundredth birthday; and her Theresienstadt poems were only discovered after Walter's death. As the number of survivors who can talk about Nazi genocide dwindles, the importance of the writing they left us increases. I believe that translating my great-aunt's work is an essential act of witness.

The word *Glimmer* recurs frequently in Rose Scooler's poems. It is the German word for mica. Her work offers us a glimmer, briefly lets us enter a world from which many never found their way out.

Hunger

Wir haben gehungert in bitterer Pein.
Wovon denn auch sollte gesättigt man sei?
Das Schüsselchen Suppe? Der einzige Kloss?
Das liess ja den Hunger erst recht werden gross.
Wir standen um Nachschub und werden ganz matt.
Wir standen drei Stunden und werden nicht satt.

Wir haben gehungert in bitterer Not,
Wie lange denn reichte das wenige Brot?
Dan hiess es: "Ja, Brot könnt ihr haben wohl hier,
Doch gebt Margarine, gebt Zucker dafür.
Gebt Kleider und Schuhe, – was jeder nur hat!"
Wir gaben das alles und wurden nicht satt.

Wir haben gehungert in bitterer Qual,
Wir suchten im Bunker so manch liebes Mal
Nach Abfall und Schalen, nach Blättern von Kraut
Und haben uns niemals vor etwas gegraut.
Wir putzten es ab und verzehrten es glatt,
Nichts wurde verschmäht, doch wir wurden nicht satt!

Our Hunger

We have been hungry. We were in distress.
And what food did they provide to comfort us?
One single dumpling. Thin soup – just half a bowl.
Enough nourishment to make our cravings grow.
We stand in line for three hours. Half-dead
on our feet, we wait. We are not well fed.

We have been hungry. We swallowed distrust.
Because how long do you last on pride and a crust?
And they went, 'Yes, help yourself to a loaf.
Have some margarine, some sugar. You can take both
in exchange for shoes and clothes.' That's what they said.
We surrender possessions. We are not well fed.

We have been hungry. We experienced pain
Each day we ransacked the shelter, looking again
and again for cabbage leaves, peelings, scraps.
We counted ourselves lucky to find any of that.
Cleaning up, polishing off every last shred.
Not one crumb gets rejected. We are not well fed.

Letters to the Editor

Don Paterson claims that "the musical setting of poems is almost invariably a redundant or destructive enterprise, resulting in either the contradiction of the original music, or its melodramatic duplication [...]". In which case it seems fair to ask whether he's listened to Britten's setting of Blake's Songs, to the various settings of poems by that group of early 20th-century English composers who included Gurney, Howells, Butterworth, Warlock and, especially, Finzi, (try Finzi's setting of Hardy's 'To Lizbie Brown'), whether he knows Theodorakis's settings of his friend Ritsos and of numerous other Greek poets, or the work of other modern Greek composers and their setting of Greek poets? And that's just for starters.

JOHN LUCAS, NOTTINGHAM

"Song, though, is a uniquely human business."
(Don Paterson, *Poetry Review*, Summer 2007)

Have you told the blackbird
Who wanders air
On walnuts by the yard
The rough farm where
Pines sigh above the gun's reach, or
In lilacs by our workshop's broken door?

As the sparks leap and fade
He tries and trails
A note, a run, a glide,
As one sun fails
He steals, then builds; long runs; a phrase
From brother's, father's, grandfather's lit days.

He will not cough or croup
He pours each note
Lost trees, each sweep and swoop
Gold from his throat.

ALISON BRACKENBURY, CHELTENHAM

CONTRIBUTORS

Fred D'Aguiar's first collection won the Malcolm X Prize for Poetry and the Guyana Poetry Prize; his first novel won the David Higham Prize and the Whitbread First Novel Award. His twelve volumes now include *An English Sampler: New and Selected Poems* (Chatto, 2003).

Mehdi Akhayan-Saales (1928-1990) first came to prominence with *Winter / Zemestan*, published after his period as a political prisoner in the 1950s.

Ali Alizadeh is an award-winning Iranian-born Australian poet, critic and literary translator. His latest collection is *Eyes in Times of War* (Salt, 2006).

Attar: Farid od-Din "Attar of Neishpour" (c.1124–1220) was a herbalist and healer who made a critical contribution to the development of Persian mystical poetry.

Ros Barber's second collection, *Material*, will be published by Anvil in 2008.

Kate Bingham's *Quicksand Beach* (Seren, 2006) was short-listed for the Forward Prize.

Peter Bland was associated with the Wellington Group and, when he returned to the UK in 1970, with London Magazine. Carcanet publish his *Collected Poems*.

Alan Brownjohn's latest volume is *Collected Poems* (Enitharmon, 2006).

Jane Draycott has recently been writer-in-residence at Henley's River and Rowing Museum and Royal Literary Fund Fellow at the Oxford Brookes Poetry Centre.

Adam Elgar lives in Bristol. He has worked as a schoolteacher.

Carrie Etter teaches at Bath Spa University. Her reviews and poems have appeared in the *TLS*.

Ruth Fainlight's most recent collection is *Moon Wheels* (Bloodaxe, 2006).

Kit Fan was born in Hong Kong. He is currently translating Confucius and Tu Fu, among other Tang poets.

Elaine Feinstein's latest collection is *Talking to the Dead* (Carcanet, 2006).

Andrew Fentham was born in Birmingham in 1986.

Sarah Hannah had a PhD from Columbia University and taught at Emerson College. Her second, posthumous, collection *Inflorescence* (Tupelo Press, Dorset, Vermont) is due out this autumn. These poems are used with permission of the Sarah Hannah Estate.

Martin Harrison's *Selected Poems* will appear next year from University of Western Australia Press, Australia/Shearsman, UK. This poem first appeared in ed. Dorothy Porter, *The Best Australian Poems 2006*, Black Inc, Melbourne.

David Harsent's *Selected Poems* (Faber, 2007) is a PBS Recommendation.

Inna Lisnianskaya's *Far from Sodom*, a selection edited and translated by Daniel Weissbort, was published by Arc in 2005.

John Kinsella's latest books include the *New Arcadia* (Norton, 2006) and *Peripheral Light: New and Selected Poems* (Norton, 2006). He is a Fellow of Churchill College, Cambridge.

Robert Littman is Professor of Classics at the University of Hawaii.

E.A.Markham's fiction, *At Home with Miss Vanesa* (Tindal Street Press) was published in 2006.

Donovan McAbee, a licensed Baptist minister from South Carolina, is studying for a PhD at the University of St Andrews.

Thomas McCarthy's latest collection is *Merchant Prince* (Anvil, 2005). He has won the Patrick Kavangh Award, the American-Irish Foundation's Literary Award and the O'Shaughnessy Prize.

Peter McDonald's latest collection is *The House of Clay* (Carcanet 2007). He is also the editor of Louis MacNeice, *Collected Poems* (Faber, 2007).

Jamie McKendrick's review of recent German translations appears on pp.90–93.

Nigel McLoughlin is Principal Lecturer in Creative Writing at the University of Gloucestershire. His fourth poetry collection, *Dissonances*, is just out from Bluechrome.

Andrew Mitchell lives and works on Lewis.

David Morley is Professor of Creative Writing at the University of Warwick and author of *The Cambridge Introduction to Creative Writing* (CUP, 2007).

Alice Oswald's *Woods, etc* (Faber, 2005) was short-listed for the Forward and T.S.Eliot Prizes.

Don Paterson's *Orpheus* appeared in 2006. *Landing Light* (2003) won the T.S.Eliot and Whitbread Prizes.

Robin Robertson's latest collection, *Swithering*, was a PBS Choice and won the 2006 Forward Prize.

Sibyl Ruth's most recent collection is *I Could Become That Woman* (Five Leaves).

Eva Salzman's *Double Crossing: New and Selected Poems* (Bloodaxe, 2004) was a PBS Recommendation, as was her first collection.

Vernon Scannell is a poet and (retired) boxer. He has won the Cholmondely and Heinemann Awards and is an Honorary Fellow of the Royal Society of Literature.

Charles Simic is the fifteenth Poet Laureate of the United States and a Poetry Editor of the *Paris Review*. He received the 2007 Wallace Stevens Award of the Academy of American Poets.

Simon Smith is Senior Lecturer in Creative Writing at London South Bank

University; Salt publishes his latest collection of poetry, *Mercury* (2006).

Janet Sutherland's *Burning the Heartwood* (2006) is published by Shearsman Press.

Charles Tomlinson's latest book of poems was *Cracks in the Universe* (Carcanet, 2006)

Christopher Wallace-Crabbe is Emeritus Professor at the University of Melbourne. Among his more than twenty books is the "rope of stories" *The Universe Looks Down* (Brandl and Schlesinger, 2005).

Daniel Weissbort edited *Selected Translations of Ted Hughes* (Faber, 2006). He is a Fellow of King's College, London and Honorary Professor at Warwick University.

David Wheatley's latest book is Mocker (Gallery Press).

John Whitworth's sonnet history was a regular feature of *Poetry Review* in the 1990s.

ß

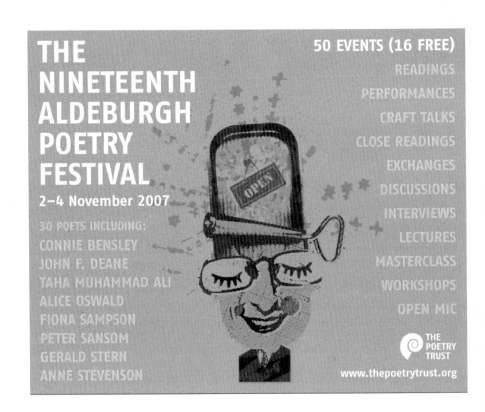